Verbivoracious Press

Festschrift Volume Three

THE

SYLLABUS

VP Festschrift Series:

Volume 1: Christine Brooke-Rose
Volume 2: Gilbert Adair
Volume 3: The Syllabus
(Edited by G.N. Forester and M.J. Nicholls)

Reprint Titles:

The Languages of Love
The Sycamore Tree
The Dear Deceit
The Middlemen
Go When You See the Green Man Walking
Next
Xorandor/Verbivore
by Christine Brooke-Rose

Three Novels — Rosalyn Drexler
Knut — Tom Mallin
Erowina — Tom Mallin

other Verbivoracious titles @

www.verbivoraciouspress.org

Verbivoracious Press

Festschrift Volume Three

edited by G.N. Forester and M.J. Nicholls

THE
SYLLABUS

"We must take our sentences seriously, which means we must understand them philosophically, and the odd thing is that the few who do, who take them with utter sober seriousness, the utter sober seriousness of right-wing parsons and political saviors, the owners of Pomeranians, are the liars who want to be believed, the novelists and poets, who know that the creatures they imagine have no other being than the sounding syllables which the reader will speak into his own weary and distracted head. There are no magic words. To say the words is magical enough."
—William H. Gass

Verbivoracious Press

Glentrees, 13 Mt Sinai Lane, Singapore

First published in Great Britain and Singapore

by Verbivoracious Press

www.verbivoraciouspress.org

Copyright (c) 2015 Verbivoracious Press

Text Copyright (c) 2015 Authors Listed Herein

Art Copyright (c) 2015 Silvia Barlaam

All rights reserved. No part of this publication may be reproduced, stored in an electronic or otherwise retrieval system, or transmitted in any form or by any means, electronic, mechanical, digital imaging, recording, otherwise, without the prior consent of the publisher.

The Authors herein assert the moral right to be identified as author of their respective contributions to this work.

ISBN: 978-981-09-3593-1

Printed and bound in Great Britain and Singapore

Contents

Introduction or, The Art of Sillybustering   1
Editors

Jonathan Swift — A Modest Proposal [1729]   3
Scott Beauchamp

Laurence Sterne — The Life and Opinions of Tristram Shandy [1759]   5
Silvia Barlaam

Xiao Hong (萧红) — The Field of Life and Death [1935]   7
Wee Teck Lim

Louis-Ferdinand Céline — Death on the Installment Plan [1936]   10
Paul John Adams

Rayner Heppenstall — The Blaze of Noon [1939]   12
Juliet Jacques

James Joyce — Finnegans Wake [1939]   14
Fionnuala Nic Mheanmán

Flann O'Brien — At Swim-Two-Birds [1939]   20
Edwin Turner

Raymond Queneau — Exercises in Style [1947]   22
Geoff Wilt

Boris Vian — Foam of the Daze [1947]   24
Tosh Berman

Douglas Woolf — The Hypocritic Days [1955]   26
Ammiel Alcalay

Henry Miller — Quiet Days in Clichy [1956]   28
G.N. Forester

Muriel Spark — *The Comforters* [1957]   30
Kim Fay

Alexander Trocchi — *Cain's Book* [1960]   32
Gill Tasker

Michel Butor — *Mobile* [1962]   34
John Trefry

Robert Pinget — *The Inquisitory* [1962]   36
? ? ?

B.S. Johnson — *Omnibus* [1964-1971]   38
Nicolas Tredell

Raymond Queneau — *The Blue Flowers* [1965]   40
Inez Hedges

Alan Burns — *Celebrations* [1967]   42
Joseph Andrew Darlington

Guillermo Cabrera Infante — *Three Trapped Tigers* [1967]   45
Pablo Medina

Macedonia Fernández—*The Museum of Eterna's Novel* [1967]   47
Steve Penkevich

Anna Kavan — *Ice* [1967]   49
Kristine Rabberman

J.M.G Le Clézio — *Terra Amata* [1967]   51
Keith Moser

Flann O'Brien — *The Third Policeman* [1967]   53
Alex Johnston

Ishmael Reed—*The Freelance Pallbearers* [1967]   55
Joseph McGrath

Christine Brooke-Rose — *Between* [1968]   57
Katarzyna Bartoszyńska

Anthony Earnshaw & Eric Thacker — *Musrum* [1968]   59
Kenneth Cox

Nicholas Mosley — Impossible Object [1968]   61
Shiva Rahbaran

Vladimir Nabokov — Ada or Ardor [1969]   63
Rob Friel

J.G. Ballard — The Atrocity Exhibition [1970]   65
Rick McGrath

Pierre Guyotat — Eden Eden Eden [1970]   68
Peter Blundell

Raymond Federman — Double or Nothing [1971]   70
Lance Olsen

Hubert Selby Jnr. — The Room [1971]   72
Georgina Holland

Stanley Crawford — Log of the S.S. the Mrs Unguentine [1972]   74
Stephen Sparks

Tom Mallin — Erowina [1972]   76
Nate Dorr

Ann Quin — Tripticks [1972]   78
Francis Booth

Guy Davenport — Taitlin! [1974]   80
Eric Byrd

Lawrence Durrell — The Avignon Quintet [1974-1985]   82
Nadine Mainard

Chrisine Brooke-Rose — Thru [1975]   87
David Detrich

Georges Perec — An Attempt at Exhausting a Place in Paris [1975]   89
Lauren Elkin

Fernando del Paso — Palinuro of Mexico [1976]   91
Ignacio M. Sánchez Prado

Coleman Dowell — Island People [1976]   93
Eugene H. Hayworth

Raymond Federman — Take It or Leave It [1976]   96
Steve Katz

Italo Calvino — If on a winter's night a traveller [1979]   99
Silvia Barlaam

Gilbert Sorrentino — Mulligan Stew [1979]   101
M.J. Nicholls

Roald Dahl — The Twits [1980]   103
Harold Lad

Donald Barthelme — Sixty Stories [1981]   105
Lee Klein

Alexander Theroux — Darconville's Cat [1981]   107
Steven Moore

Camilo José Cela — Mrs. Caldwell Speaks to Her Son [1982]   109
Rosalyn Drexler

D. Keith Mano — Take Five [1982]   112
Nathan Gaddis

Thomas Bernhard — Woodcutters [1984]   114
Anonymous

Christine Brooke-Rose — Amalgamemnon [1984]   116
Ellen G. Friedman

Rikki Ducornet — The Stain [1984]   119
Michelle Ryan-Sautour

Christoph Meckel — The Figure on the Boundary Line [1984]   121
Ben Winch

Milorad Pavić — Dictionary of the Khazars (Male Edition) [1984]   123
Alec Nevala-Lee

Milorad Pavić — Dictionary of the Khazars (Female Edition) [1984]   125
Silvia Barlaam

Don Delillo — White Noise [1985]   127
Barbara Melville

Gilbert Sorrentino — Pack of Lies Trilogy [1985-1989]   129
Dick Witherspoon

Ronald Sukenick — In Form: Digressions on the Act of Fiction [1985]   131
Tom Willard

Marcel Bénabou — Why I Have Not Written Any of My Books [1986]   133
A. Writer

Michael Westlake — Imaginary Women [1987]   135
Michael Westlake

Nicholson Baker — The Mezzanine [1988]   137
M.J. Nicholls

Italo Calvino — Six Memos for the Next Millennium [1988]   139
Daniel Levin Becker

David Markson — Wittgenstein's Mistress [1988]   141
Christopher WunderLee

Janice Galloway — The Trick is to Keep Breathing [1989]   143
Gillian Devine

Jacques Roubaud — The Great Fire of London [1989]   145
Ian Monk

Felipe Alfau — Chromos [1990]   147
Sam Moss

Robert Alan Jamieson — A Day at the Office [1991]   149
Rodge Glass

Alasdair Gray — Poor Things [1992]   151
Rodge Glass

W.G. Sebald — The Emigrants [1992]   153
Peter Bebergal

William Gaddis — A Frolic of His Own [1994]   155
Christopher WunderLee

Jáchym Topol — City Sister Silver [1994]   157
Alex Zucker

Martin Amis — *The Information* [1995]   160
Anthony Vacca

William H. Gass — *The Tunnel* [1995]   162
H.L. Hix

Gilbert Sorrentino — *Red the Fiend* [1995]   164
Jenny Offill

Roberto Bolaño — *Nazi Literature in the Americas* [1996]   167
Adrian Carney

Geoff Dyer — *Out of Sheer Rage* [1997]   169
Kathleen Heil

Alasdair Brotchie & Harry Mathews (eds.) — *Oulipo Compendium* [1998]   171
Jason Graff

Dubravka Ugrešić — *The Museum of Unconditional Surrender* [1998]   173
Jasmina Lukić

Percival Everett — *Glyph* [1999]   175
Tom Conoboy

Ali Smith — *Other Stories and Other Stories* [1999]   177
M.J. Nicholls

Ignácio de Loloya Brandão — *Anonymous Celebrity* [2002]   179
Ricki Aklon

Curtis White — *Requiem* [2002]   181
Trevor Dodge

Lucy Ellmann — *Dot in the Universe* [2003]   183
Ali Millar

Dubravka Ugrešić — *Thank You for Not Reading* [2003]   185
Ana Stanojevic

Roberto Bolaño — *2666* [2004]   187
Alex Cox

Meredith Brosnan — *Mr. Dynamite* [2004]   189
Jarleth L. Prendergast

David Mitchell — Cloud Atlas [2004] 192
Stephen Mirabito

Steve Katz — Antonello's Lion [2005] 194
W.C. Bamberger

Graham Rawle — Woman's World [2005] 196
Michael Leong

Gilbert Adair — The Evadne Mount Trilogy [2006-2009] 198
Manny Rayner

Nicola Barker — Darkmans [2007] 201
Kinga Burger

Lydia Davis — Varieties of Disturbance [2007] 203
Ali Millar

Lydie Salvayre — Portrait of the Writer as a Domesticated Animal [2007] 205
Juliet Jacques

Adam Thirwell — Miss Herbert [2007] 207
Jack Ross

Urmuz — Collected Works [2007] 209
Eddie Watkins

Marilyn Chin — Revenge of the Mooncake Vixen [2009] 211
Melanie Ho

Gabriel Josipovici — Only Joking [2010] 213
Gianni Dane

Steven Moore — The Novel: An Alternative History [2010-2013] 216
Nathan Gaddis

Will Self — Walking to Hollywood [2010] 218
Richard Strachan

Charles Newman — In Partial Disgrace [2013] 220
Eric Lundgren

The Influences of Others 222
Igo Wodan

Introduction or, The Art of Sillybustering

EDITORS

The concept of a public list sanctioning the Best and Most Essential Books constitutes an artistic stranglehold and an unforgivable infringement on one's reading freedom. If readers accept at face value an 100 Best Books list and proceed to wade through the familiar mishmash of the canonical, popular modern classics, and uninspired editor's preferences as the Best Books on offer, once again a whole universe of exploratory, unusual, ill-fitting-to-a-marketeer's-category literature is marginalised as marginalia. The (dubious) pleasure in these lists lies in detecting the compilers' motives behind some of the less familiar choices or, on rare occasions, alighting upon an unfamiliar choice worth reading. Online magazine *38 Pitches* lists books as strange as *But Is It True?: A Citizen's Guide to Environmental Health and Safety Issues* by Aaron Wildavsky, a 586-page academic text published in 1995, alongside *Jefferson and His Times* by Dumas Malone, and the list unfurls a bias towards historical and social American novels with lazy pokes of F5 for the classics. Amazon's list as predicted is compiled with algorithmic precision towards the mass market, thus sits *The Diary of Anne Frank* above *The Fault in Our Stars* without a single forehead being wrinkled. *The Telegraph* (UK) is the blandest of the bunch and dares to place *Atonement* before *Life: A User's Manual*, while *The Guardian* has a list concocted by Norwegian book clubs(!) who asked "54 countries around the world to nominate the ten books which have had the most decisive impact on the cultural history of the world."[1] As a consequence, the list is a pangalactic splattergun encompassing *The Tale of Genji*, *Njal's Saga*, *Mahabharata*, and *The Book of Job* (still making room for *1984* and *To the Lighthouse*).

---

[1] http://www.theguardian.com/world/2002/may/08/books.booksnews

The third VP festschrift is not a 100 Best Books list (nor is it technically a festschrift, although we are *festing* these books and short *schrifting* the clichés), it is a Syllabus, meaning we have chosen the books listed based on our personal preferences for vocabularic pyrotechnics, astounding assonance and/or alliterative alliteration, grammatical gadgetry, form begetting content, structural innovation, and general genius, not to mention our contributors' hagglings for alternative titles to those suggested, and whether we had short pieces about these books on hand (as opposed to any other limb) in the event of a contributor drought.

As a publisher devoted to the more outré of the avant-garde, many of the selections belong to this tradition, with the occasional exception as a desperate if futile gesture aiming at mass-market acceptance and this book being included in the next Amazon list above *The Lost Symbol* and *Are You There God? It's Me, Margaret*. Each contributor was asked to write a 500-word creative response to her/his selected text—a short primer, a mini-essay, a microfiction, or any inspired inventive formal imitation. The results are this all-star bumper crop of treats and a panoply of texts, which once imbibed will induce in the reader a state of literary euphoria, or your festschrift cost will be refunded.[2] The process for selection was a fraught experience requiring two weeks of intensive debate, pen wrestling, and at one point, an obscure round of tossing greens (G.N. Forester excelled at flinging fresh bulbs of fennel at a dartboard—as a consequence *The Avignon Quintet* has been included). Please revel in this scintillating revue of texts and afterwards place a few of these generally neglected works on your to-read lists.

---

2 Not a promise.

Jonathan Swift — A Modest Proposal [1729]

SCOTT BEAUCHAMP

MODEST OBSTACLES AND EXTRAVAGANT OPPORTUNITIES: A TED TALK

Can you all hear me?
Great. I want to apologize in advance if I seem uncomfortable wearing a headset. This is my first talk like this and I'm not quite used to the equipment.

I want to speak with you today about two things. One: My identity as a businessman—or as I like to call it, a happiness producer. The other is Maria. Maria is my neighbor, in a way. She shares the streets and parks of my hometown of Jacksonville, Florida. She requires at least as much caloric intake as me, possibly more if you consider her three children. But Maria doesn't produce anything. While I work, sometimes 12 hours a day, at my marketing firm, Consumer Outreach Solutions, harnessing the awesome and revolutionary power of social networking technology to build markets for customers and customers for markets, Maria sits on the corner of Delgado and Union Streets hoping to beg a dollar or two from a motorist pausing at a red light.

I don't know Maria's story. I don't know how she found herself one day at an intersection begging for change. And I used to think of her as a tragedy. And her kids? Even more so. And so one day, as my car engine idled at a red light, as I was absentmindedly sipping a coffee and staring at Maria, a revolutionary idea came to me: in order to produce the greatest amount of happiness for the greatest number of people, we need to utilize Maria and her children. We need them, instead of taking

—and suffering, I might add—we need them to become producers of contentment.

Maria doesn't have a useful education. She probably never graduated from high school. Her children, as we know all too well, are more likely to end up dead or in jail than to create a revolutionary start-up or join an investment firm. We need to utilize the strengths that they DO have: energy. The human body is an energy machine. Our movement, our heat, even our mass is potential energy. While I'm in the office strategizing innovative ways to bring customers to life-changing products, Maria and her children could be busy holding up their end too and, say, producing the energy to run my computer, light my office, and cool me off in the hot summer days. If we could bring corporate sponsorship into this, a bargain between business and the less than fortunate who fill our cities, we could even create a program where Maria is compensated in corporate deals and merchandise for the energy she creates.

Here's an example: Coca-Cola sponsors Maria. She earns points by spending time in a kinetic collection and tank (and yes, the technology is available). For their part, Coca-Cola compensates Maria with merchandise: blankets, soda, t-shirts, sunglasses. And her children can join in too: stuffed animals, candy, toys that are connected to specific corporate campaigns. Everyone wins.

Laurence Sterne — The Life and Opinions of Tristram Shandy, Gentleman [1759]

SILVIA BARLAAM

First, a blank page, to signify the open invitation to go forwards, to read whatever sign has not yet been written, the offer of a space wherein the reader can ink her own words and meaning. Or a black page, instead, so much felt that too many words would not be enough and just overlap with each other—the difference between pages being a small letter, just 'n'. What else can we deduce from the importance of a single letter, or where can we go from a consideration of the alphabet and the phonetic system, to how I learned to speak as a child and the reproduction of sounds by the laws of physics, and furthermore, onwards, to a disquisition on the sciences and literature and personal reminiscences and travelling and meetings of minds and people.

If I were to say, one book, choose now, it would probably be this one. It goes everywhere but where it is supposed to, it is an unruly woollen thread spreading all over the (imaginary?) place, following alleys and main roads and opening doors long forgotten ajar and climbing steps leading to basements.

This book surprises you and engages you, yes, you, the reader, it challenges you with questions, requires your presence of mind, your intellect, to engage with the pages and words and visuals—only limited to what the printing press could achieve in 1759, an innovation in what a book, a novel, could be.

Before I tell you more about this book, let me say that reading a book, any book, is an adventure, wading through words and sentences and paragraphs, figuring out who's who and why and what and when and how, finding the context, cultural and historical and hysterical—

possibly not the latter, but why not—is there a message, a theme, a topic? Is the author's voice hidden behind the pages, or buttered all over them? Does the writer's preoccupation with structure, ideas and characterization come through? Is there sweat dripping off the corner of the cover?

Is it, all and any of the above, important? And why am I here, telling you about this particular book of all available books, what prompted me on this road, put a pen—not anymore, it is my fingers flying on this keyboard—and what is the difference between the virtual and the ink, the press and the page versus the publisher and the e-reader?

This is what is like reading *Tristram Shandy*: going everywhere, on a journey, starting from so many different directions, learning by glancing aside, being showered on from above, rolling in an old cart while listening to a witty, intelligent, amusing storyteller and being shown the many ways in which ink can animate a page.

Xiao Hong (萧红) — *The Field of Life and Death* [1935]

WEE TECK LIM

THE NOVELIST AS ETHNOGRAPHER

The choice of Xiao Hong (萧红) for this festschrift as an example of an overlooked writer may seem strange when two films about her life have recently been released on the back of the 100th anniversary of her death—Huo Jianqi's *Falling Flowers* (<<萧红>>) in 2012 and, to greater acclaim, Ann Hui's *The Golden Era* (<<黄金时代>>) in 2014. However, while she is not unknown in China, her name and her works remain largely unknown in the Western literary world.

It also seems strange to accredit her with being an exploratory writer in this postmodernist age given that she wrote "realist" fiction. Here, my justification is somewhat more suspect. It is true that she wrote not in high literary Chinese but in the vernacular, and to understand just how much a break with the past that was in 1920s China, imagine if you will that English literature had gone from Shakespeare to Hemingway overnight. It is also true that she was one of the earliest practitioners of the Chinese realist novel. However, all great artists have at their time struck out into the unknown: the fate of all innovation is to become part of the mundane.

However, as an inspiration of what great novels can aspire to, it seems to me that Xiao Hong's greatest works, her first novel—*The Field of Life and Death* (<<生死>>)—and her last—*Tales of Hulan River* (<<呼兰河传>>), bring something to the literary table that I have not encountered anywhere else: what she gives us is a depiction of a community, the novel as ethnography. For all the individual stories that she tells in these works, their beating heart is the Harbin community in which she grew up. As Howard Goldblatt notes in his introduction to his translation of her work, "*The Field of Life and Death* is not the story of any particular individual . . . It is the aggregate village that has the starring role, and with the author's skill, it comes alive."

Like a carpet weaver, Xiao Hong keeps us always aware of the larger socio-economic and cultural pattern in which her vignettes occur even as she focuses on the specific details of an incident or of a life. On the one hand, she is not writing a story focused on the dramatic arcs of individual lives with their beginning, middles, and ends; on the other hand, the colour and specificity that she gives to her characters and their lives gives these portraits sufficient individuality that they become more than mere representations.

The Field of Life and Death follows the lives of various persons in a village in northern China. Events play out over a period of a few years, beginning before the Japanese invasion of Manchuria and ending during the occupation years. Through a series of vignettes, Xiao Hong builds up a picture of the harsh, rural lives of the peasants: a villager who loses his ox has to be his own draught animal; a paraplegic woman is abandoned by her husband to die in her own excrement; an old horse has to be sold to pay the rent; a woman seeking work in the city has to resort to prostitution after the little she has saved from doing piecework is stolen. In the end, what we are left with is not so much individual tales but the story of the village and its villagers.

In *Tales of Hulan River*, Xiao Hong uses the same approach to paint a picture of the village in which she grew up as the daughter of a rich merchant among the poor peasants. By then, her craft has matured and she deftly interweaves details both comic and tragic, such as a scene where an itinerant peddler of dough sticks visits a house of five children, and the squabbling amongst the children over who gets what rapidly descends to Keystone cop territory. Scenes such as these, however, take place alongside a story of a child bride who, subjected to a brutal cure for demon possession, is boiled alive. And amongst such tales are also descriptions of village festivals or, quite simply, the flaming red sunsets that constituted entertainment for the deprived villagers.

One might object that there is nothing unique in what she has done, pointing to works like Gabriel Garcia Marquez's *One Hundred Years of Solitude* or Vikram Seth's *A Suitable Boy*. However, Marquez's Maconda and the people remain representations throughout, and never a specific village or individual. On the same side of the line would fall Salman Rushdie's *Midnight's Children* or Joshua Ferris' *Then We Came to the End*. In Seth's *A Suitable Boy*, it is the stories of Lata, Haresh, and Maan that take centre stage. The beginnings, middles, and ends of their love lives and struggles are what animate the novel, even as Seth intersperses these with the historical events of their times. In this category would fall works like Tolstoy's *War and Peace* and Armistead Maupin's *Tales of the City*.

To me, this is a path that the modern novel might have taken but has eschewed: the stories of communities (whether a village, an office or profession, or a city) embedded not in individual dramas but in the living, breathing ebb and flow of the communities themselves. Surely there is room that kind of novel too?

Louis-Ferdinand Céline — Death on the Installment Plan [1936]

PAUL JOHN ADAMS

If your idea of a good time is cartloads of pricks and balls and mountains of flayed, bloody flesh, then you're in for a treat with *Death on the Installment Plan*. "*The women's dresses are in tatters, tits torn and dangling... little boys without pants... they knock each other down, trample each other, toss each other up in the air... some are left dangling from the trees... along with smashed up chairs.*" Controlling idea? Everything is ugly, everything is hell. The novel is extremely disorienting, like everything Céline wrote. It's vulgar and anarchic. You're plunged into the misery and anxiety of an older Ferdinand, cynical beyond compare, raving at times . . . a charity doctor! And before you get your bearings, and you've flown through thirty or forty pages of filthy patients and gang rape, just as you're getting the idea that this guy's noble deed is to sustain the lives of murderers and syphilitic whores long enough that they can spread their violence and infection, just as the protagonist's chronic tinnitus and some ungodly illness cause his world to really explode in a fountain of shit and vomit, marching soldiers, roving bands of masturbators and heaped up corpses . . . well, just about then the novel *starts* and you didn't even realize you were only in a kind of "present" prologue that's setting you up to experience the hell of childhood. A comic tale of perpetual abuse and humiliation! What can we really expect for a naïve and innocent suffering whelp with a permanently shitty ass who's born into a family of brutes, vagabonds, philanderers, murdered prostitutes and suicides, all preoccupied in their life with scraping up enough sous to buy a few noodles? Well . . . not much good. One of the two great classic novels in which a character vomits into another's mouth! Here we are at the turn of the century (19th to 20th), an exciting time full of possibility, when bicycles and lighter-than-air vehicles promise to revolutionize transport (and make the airplane obsolete), when electrical wires under the soil are bound to make potatoes grow at a miraculous rate. Everyone's a con, everyone's a charlatan, everyone's ready to try to get over by selling out whatever sucker is fool enough to trust. "*Kidnapping... moral turpitude... obscene practices... illegal gambling... fraudulent tax returns... vice... burglary... abuse of confidence... nocturnal marauding... concealment of minors*" . . . why not? Ferdinand's out to break your heart, if you have a heart. Don't believe it when he says of a woman "*She took the lowest view and she was right.*" He's anxious and terrified but he's not so jaded . . . this proposed defense doesn't work. If you feel revulsion and horror, believe it, he knows he's taken you there and he's felt it too. "*Life has nothing to do with feelings.*" Lies, I tell you! There's a soul in this novel, there's empathy (not spoken, not always on the page . . . but in you!), there's hope and a flickering awareness of what beauty may reside in our dreams, but that soul is a suffering bastard, and that hope is born to sputter out. This world pisses on our childhood and our dreams. Miserable little Ferdinand, now I know how you got from there to here. The prologue is your destiny, but not your ultimate destiny . . . that's death . . . waiting to tear your guts out through your whining, simpering mouth if they don't come out your ass first.

Rayner Heppenstall — The Blaze of Noon [1939]

JULIET JACQUES

Since the late D. H. Lawrence's banned book, "Lady Chatterley's Lover", no novel has been published in this country so boldly challenging the censor by its frank dealing with sex matters as "The Blaze of Noon" by Mr. Rayner Heppenstall ...

So began *The Evening Standard*'s review of Heppenstall's debut novel, published by Secker & Warburg in November 1939, two months into the Second World War. Without the paper branding it 'an affront to decency', *The Blaze of Noon* may have vanished entirely (a fate that awaited Heppenstall's brilliant follow-up *Saturnine*)—as it happened, their outrage ensured that it sold out immediately, but masked its literary qualities, despite Elizabeth Bowen's subtle, sensitive foreword.

Aged 28, Heppenstall had moved from Huddersfield to London, working as a cultural critic and living with Irish author Michael Sayers. In his memoirs, Heppenstall said that Sayers told him that 'you could never write a novel': *The Blaze of Noon* was his attempt to prove Sayers wrong, in which he used the blind masseur visiting Sayers' mother as the starting point for a first-person narrative.

More serious reviewers than the *Standard*'s, noting the amount of sex in the novel, compared Heppenstall to DH Lawrence and Henry Miller, but Bowen correctly identified Heppenstall's main influences as French, calling *The Blaze of Noon* 'a novel one might imagine being written ten, or even twenty years hence.' Certainly, it was far from the socially engaged British works of the Depression, due to Heppenstall's belief that 'film had assumed the novel's exteriorised narrative function' so that literary prose should 'become more lyrical, more inward'. What really distinguished it, however, were the extensive descriptions of the physical properties of objects, including other people, and speculation upon their meanings and motives, as narrator Louis Dunkel struggled to compensate for his sightlessness.

This experimentation, with the boundaries between Dunkel's interior consciousness and the outside world becoming unclear, led some critics to name *The Blaze of Noon* as the founding work of the *nouveau roman*—most notably Hélène Cixous in *Le Monde* in 1967. Heppenstall, always self-effacing, said he did not belief that Alain Robbe-Grillet, Nathalie Sarraute or any other post-war French Modernists read it, even in translation, feeling that a shared set of influences, particularly right-wing authors such as Louis-Ferdinand Céline and Henry de Montherlant, accounted for the structural similarities.

The Blaze of Noon slipped in and out of print, being reissued in 1967 and then 1980, a year before Heppenstall's death. Then, Julian Symons called it 'an orthodox novel . . . about sex', but actually it was a critique of bourgeois sexual morals, and their fragility. Not always reliably, Dunkel recounts the recriminations that follow his arrival, and how his affairs disrupt the hosting family, in lucid, poetic prose, blaming his own reading of Nietzsche for his selfishness before questioning his own position as narrator. He stops just short of admitting that this has been bestowed by an author, and it was left to Heppenstall's post-war successors to write works that pulled themselves apart so explicitly, but his was a ground-breaking novel, and one that is—happily—now back in print.

James Joyce — Finnegans Wake [1939]

FIONNUALA NIC MHEANMÁN

THE SLALOM OF JOYLEDGE

Howto scaledown this Beschova finntail
This filletof beginnings that sings of all endings,
This pest of a pal in jest
And bad cess to you, Joyking
For the reeding is *tuff tuff*
But the prize is the *laffing*
Tho *low* in the belly
It sores with the learning
Of finnglish and *jinglish*
Pigeon *linguish* and *djoytisch*

Ten stories tall
And twenty the *deepings*
some to the writeof
And Moore to the *leftings*
Finn's *houseful* of hawsers
And *hods* and their *spilling*
Give *Humpty* his tallwall
And role in all fallings
Atomnal, Printernal
Summerian, Hibernial

Story forth into *bygones*

O Joyking of spieling
Ewe raddle us with riddles
Till we're red in the *blushers*
Veins *vulg*ing in temples
And grey matter smarting
We *reed* in the *rushes*
Of joycfull *mehind*ing
Seepon, seepunder,
pong of pondyman

Thru *hart* strings and wordlings
And lingo lang twanging
Ewe bleat all the sorrel
Of wars evel waging
In valleys, on hillsides
In shore water rising
But miss chiefs and piss takes
Give rest from *sorratelling*
spoofon, spoofonder,
sham of shemyman
Futurepresent pastperfect
As the river at her rising
The trees bend to bog
From the turf seeds fresh reedlings
Men breed new wars
As old wars reseeding
Bodies for battles
Procreation creating
Weepon, weeponder,
Song of sorrowmon

Atom, Eve and their childer
The first family feuding
Cain abling his sister

THE SYLLABUS

Edem for all triblings
In cest and in jest
The story ewer spouring
By yon *labious banks*
And by *perchypole sard*ing
thru *noughty times* ever
And foriver insemenating

O Batterfull of *cod*logicals
O Senchus Mór pran*K*ing
Exagminating yore *glosses*
Yore *musikers* and *blarneying*
French rhymes and Moores chimes
Jack's house ever building
Alicetella's fun essay
Swift Sternly past teaching
Reminding this *scribbler*
To finnish *voiciferating*
Nows nunc or nimmer!

Morse-erse wordybook for The Slalom of Joyledge:*

(Woordenboek: dictionary in Norse Erse)

The Salmon of Knowledge, a mythical fish, said to embody all the knowledge of the world.

Beschoff's: a fish shop in Dublin established 1913, famous for cod fillets in batter.

Bad cess to you, a curse, recalling the cess pit.

Tim Finnegan, in the ballad, Finnegan's Wake: a hod carrier on a building site who fell off a wall, died and was resurrected when whiskey accidentally fell on his lips during his wake.

Humpty Dumpty also fell off a wall.

Humphrey, the main character in the Wake, himself suffers a fall.

The Fall of Man: the ultimate fall.

Sard, reference to fish, and alternative slang for a four letter word beginning with f.

Perchypole: a fishing rod or other type of rod.

Raddle: red colouring on ewes to mark encounter by ram.

Sorrel or red clover: plant causing infertility in sheep.

---

* All words in italics occur in *Finnegans Wake*. All words underlined occur in The Slalom of Joyledge.

THE SYLLABUS

<u>Joyking</u>: King James Joyce, author of the Finnegans Wake bible of sorts.
Pranquean: Joyce's name for 16th pirate queen, Granuaile, blithe borrower from traders along the west coast of Ireland.

<u>PranKing</u>: Joyce, pirateer and *pelagiarist*, blithe borrower of words and ideas, purveyor of jests and wordplay.

The <u>Senchus Mór</u>, referred to in *Finnegans Wake*, 5th century account of the Brehon laws of Ireland, written in ancient dialect, containing later commentaries and glosses between the lines and in the margins, the perfect metaphor for *Finnegans Wake*, itself a corpus of Irish history, written in obscure dialect with commentaries throughout the text and glosses in the margins.

<u>Shem the penman</u>: Joyce's pseudonym for himself in the *Wake*. *Shem* is the brother of *Shaun* and *Izzy*, and son of *Humphrey* and *Anna*, the <u>first family</u> around which the action revolves.

Shaun: represents Irish Nationalism, inspired by the character, Shaun the Post in Dion Boucicault's 19th century play *Arrah na Pogue*.

Izzy represents:
  Isolde: legendary figure betrothed to King Mark who eloped with young Tristan
  Grainne: legendary figure betrothed to Fionn Mac Cumhal who eloped with young Diarmuid
  Deirdre of the Sorrows: princess of Ulster whose beauty caused war and destruction
  Fionnuala: daughter of the sea god Mannanán Mac Lir
  <u>Alice</u> Liddell: Lewis Carroll's young friend
  <u>Stella</u>: Esther Johnson, Jonathan *Swift*'s great love
  <u>Vanessa</u>, Esther Vanhomrigh, Swift's other love.

Anna: Anna Livia Plurabelle, the personification of the river Liffey which flows out to the sea at Dublin Bay. In the last lines of the book she becomes the sea god Mannanán's daughter, condemned to roam the Sea of Moyle for centuries.

Humphrey: personification of the Hill of Howth, a horn of land on the north edge of Dublin city which thrusts into Dublin bay. He also represents Fionn Mac Cumhal and other mythological and historical figures.

Percy French and *Thomas Moore*: two song writers whose songs recur in the text, e.g., Moore's '*Silent, O Moyle*' about the sea god's daughter's exile. Other popular songs, rhymes and doggerel occur frequently, e.g., *The House that Jack Built*.

Everything in *Finnegans Wake* has several meanings and while often camouflaged, the meaning is nevertheless reinforced through constant layering. Many things which have been said in other texts are unsaid in *Finnegans Wake*, as in taken apart, remade, further dismantled, further refurbished in a continuous cycle similar to the geological ages of the world. Joyce's text is therefore a *palimpsest* in every sense of the word, a veritable *geoglyphy* carved out of history.

Flann O'Brien — At Swim-Two-Birds [1939]

EDWIN TURNER

"Characters should be interchangeable as between one book and another," decrees the unnamed narrator of Flann O'Brien's novel *At Swim-Two-Birds*. "The entire corpus of existing literature should be regarded as a limbo from which discerning authors could draw their characters as required." *At Swim-Two-Birds* enacts this declaration, freely borrowing characters and reframing them anew in every manner of plot, scene, and caper. The vibrant storytelling threatens to overwhelm reader and narrator alike—and what a joy to be overwhelmed.

Our narrator doesn't control his stories (and storytellers) so much as he provokes them into a life of their own, one unconstrained by pre-existing conventions. He's upfront about his prejudices: "One beginning and one ending for a book was a thing I did not agree with." Characters from different eras and genres traipse freely through his porter-fueled "literary projects," rambling, converging, dissolving, and re-emerging to beget *their own* characters.

And *oh* those characters.

We meet "Pooka MacPhellimey, a member of the devil class," a thoughtful and polite hobgoblin. There's John Furriskey, who "was born at the age of twenty-five and entered the world with a memory but without a personal experience to account for it." Furriskey is the literary creation of *another* character, one Dermot Trellis, a grumpy author of conventional Westerns. There's also Finn Mac Cool, "a legendary hero of old Ireland," who thunders through the background in baroque prose, dreaming his way into the other characters' lives. He's the generative, mythical bedrock from which they might sprout. (O'Brien's Finn is the psychic twin of Joyce's Finn—*At Swim-Two-Birds* and *Finnegans Wake* were both published in 1939).

Drawn too from Irish lore's marvellous limbo is the mad king Sweeny, who's dragged into a picaresque quest by the Pooka MacPhellimey, the Good Fairy, two cowboyish thugs (or thuggish cowboys) named Slug and Shorty, and the poet Jem Casey. The strange band sets out to bequeath gifts to a newborn infant (the creation of a creation of a creation). The quest's comic bravado and slapstick rhythm recall the manic but precise energy of Buster Keaton and the linguistic brio of the Marx brothers. But sweet pathos for poor Sweeny tempers the burlesque energy, humanizing the narrative proper.

Sweeny, broken, starving, insane, and living solely on watercress, falls into despair. His troop pushes him forward with the promise of a restorative feast: "And getting around the invalid in a jabbering ring, they rubbed him and cajoled and coaxed, and plied him with honey-talk and long sweet-lilted sentences full of fine words . . ." Those fine words continue for pages. Linguistic force becomes sustenance, revitalizing Sweeny. Imagination turns into words and words turn into food and drink. And life.

Here and elsewhere in *At Swim-Two-Birds*, O'Brien channels the generative power of storytelling, revitalizing the form of the novel itself, exploding conventional contours and resynthesizing tropes into bewildering new shapes. 75 years later, *At Swim-Two-Birds* is *still* ahead of its time, provoking its readers into new ways of reading and new ways of imagining.

Raymond Queneau — Exercises in Style [1947]

GEOFF WILT

A banal scene. Paris, 192_ or 3_. At a café on the Left Bank, an ordinary looking young gentleman—neatly cropped dark hair, wire-frame glasses—sits smoking and reading James Joyce's *Ulysses*, occasionally making notations in a worn notebook open on the table beneath him. This is my dream of Raymond Queneau coming to his reckoning with Joyce. Queneau considered *Ulysses* a "magical act"; in a 1938 article he says, "I must first of all take the precaution of acknowledging my debt to English and American novelists, who taught me that there is such a thing as a technique of the novel, and most especially to Joyce." The notebook in my fictional scene is real, it is called "The Little Cyclopædia", it contains Queneau's detailed notes on reading Joyce's epic. Joyce's book, the one that so profoundly affected Queneau, is essentially a long, complex series of exercises in style.

~

There are finite ways to tell a tale, as there are finite letters in any alphabet, finite vocables to any given language. But with these limited sets of expressibles and their myriad combinations, because there is finite (life)time in which to tell, there ends up being practically countless ways a story might be told, countless ways a scene might be seen, countless ways an image might be imagined. Not only a multiplicity of modes of representation, but, since language alone determines and structures the world in which we wander, a correlative multiplicity of realities given to each of us from any particular experience.

~

A banal scene. A comic incident on a bus, and a related observation outside a train station. Queneau's *Exercises in Style* is a language experiment, an attempt at what might be accomplished with words and storytelling post-Joyce. The 99 linguistic perspectives on a single mundane event is a labyrinth-run through a kaleidoscopic lens of possible styles. He called it a linguistic "rust-remover." A call to venture inside and uncover the latencies of language. A means of rearriving at the novel after *Ulysses*, that subsumption and assimilation of the history of Western literature, that high watermark of Modernism, that culmination of the novelistic tradition. *Ulysses* represents the end of the novel, and therefore, the point of a new beginning. (Joyce's only recourse was making *Finnegans Wake*.)

~

The novel is dead. Long live the novel! The story is the way the story is told, and nothing more, because there really is no story at all. There are only our minds coming in contact with a series of events, and how that may be construed, constructed, and determined in language. Who is telling? What did they see? What modes are they using to recount what they saw? What do these modes and their words signify about the observer, the reader, the characters being created? Why do we read, other than to appreciate *style*? How do we keep storytelling, and therefore language, new, how do we keep perception, within all of its constraints, evolving, in this long process of coming-to-be?

Boris Vian — Foam of the Daze [1947]

TOSH BERMAN

ON TRANSLATION

Out of curiosity and pleasure, I read the two English language translations of Boris Vian's *L'ecume des jours* that are now on the market. *Mood Indigo* was translated in 1967 by Stanley Chapman, and my edition (TamTam Books) was translated about ten years ago. The Brian Harper translation is called *Foam of the Daze*. The original Chapman edition, *Froth on a Daydream*. Both translated titles are good, and tricky, due to the poetic title *L'écume des jours*. The edition published by FSG is called *Mood Indigo* to tie in with film by Michel Gondry—for some reason named after the original American translation that came out in the 60s, published by Grove Press. The title *Mood Indigo* is puzzling—the song *Mood Indigo* is not mentioned at all in the book nor the film, as far I remember. The song is co-written by the great Duke Ellington, who for sure has an important presence in the Vian book. There are numerous mentions of the song by Ellington called 'Chloe', which is an incredible piece of music, but also one of the main characters in the novel is named after the song.

Besides this point, both translations of the Vian novel read very well. I eschewed Chapman's translation because I felt it needed a new and fresh interpretation, and Brian Harper, an American who lives in Paris, retained all the ingredients that make the book special. Chapman is a tad playful with his translation, which works well apart from his describing the main character Colin as a "fair-headed Jean Bellpull Rondeau in a film by Jacques Goon Luddard." In the original French edition of the book, as well as in Harper's *Foam of the Daze*, the character is described as the blond actor who plays the role of Slim in *Hollywood Canteen*. The role "Slim" is played by actor Robert Hutton. That was the visual image Vian had in mind with respect to Colin (bearing in mind that *L'écume des jours* was written and published in 1947.) The film by Jean-Luc Godard (Jacques Goon Luddard) *Breathless* was shot in 1959, and came out in France in 1960. One of the other characters in the book is named Alise—Chapman renamed her "Alyssum" in *Mood Indigo* (*Froth on a Daydream*). Alyssum is a type of flower, so Chapman may have used her name as a pun, referring to the plants and flowers that are listed in the book. Another example of Chapman playing with names is the 19th century cookbook that Colin's chef-friend uses throughout the novel. Jules Gouffé was known as a great chef, and his cookbook is very well-known in France. In *Mood Indigo* the chef's name is "ffroydde", which is (or appears to be) an arcane pun of sorts. Chapman plays with titles and names throughout the book, yet his narrative style is strong. I question his choices of names and titles, when they are clearly stated in the original French text by Vian.

Foam of the Daze is based on the 1994 French edition prepared by Gilbert Rybalka and Michel Rybalka, with endnotes by those gentlemen and its translator Brian Harper. Brian also wrote a beautiful introduction to his translation. Also interesting to note is that Chapman, who is British, for sure has his national language in *Mood Indigo*, while *Foam of the Daze* is very much American English. A slight if notable difference. Vian had an appreciation for British literature (for instance, Nicolas is based partly on P.G. Wodehouse's Jeeves) and yet I feel that American English is the proper idiom in Vian's translations—especially with respect to his Vernon Sullivan novels which take place in America (when, ironically enough, Vian never visited the States). It is fun to read both translations side-by-side, and easy to do due to their short and concise chapters. Movie or no movie, it is fantastic that the Stanley Chapman translation is available—without a doubt *L'écume des jours* is an excellent book—whether translated by Chapman or Brian Harper—it's a classic and deserves an ecstatic first reading.

Douglas Woolf — The Hypocritic Days [1955]

AMMIEL ALCALAY

It's been over fifty years since then LeRoi Jones, the late Amiri Baraka, edited the remarkable prose collection *The Moderns: an anthology of new writing in America*. Outside of Jack Kerouac and William Burroughs, the prose of most of the writers included in that 1963 anthology remains, at best, neglected. As Baraka wrote in his introduction: "The possibility of a 'new American poetry' meant, of course, that there was equally to be sought out, a new or fresher American prose." But no matter what inroads to that culture of poetry have been made since, the prose remains obscure, and among the most obscure is the figure universally agreed upon by the participants in that world to be one of its acknowledged masters: Douglas Woolf. His first book, *The Hypocritic Days*, a novella titled after a line in a poem by Emerson, was published in Mallorca by Robert Creeley's Divers Press in 1955, and it is to that exquisite edition that I turn, even though it was reprinted in the 1993 Black Sparrow volume *Hypocritic Days and Other Tales*, with a preface by Edward Dorn, another ally of the times. With a striking abstract drawing in solid purple and black by Japanese poet, artist, and designer Katue Kitasono on the cover, the book was printed in an edition, as Creeley wrote, of "a few hundred copies." The novella certainly features the unsettling mix of descriptive allusion and tender absurdity that would come to characterize Woolf's depiction of ordinary life in a world gone absolutely stark raving mad. And the conditions, as indicated in the very opening of the book, are not only local: "He stepped out the door into a cooling world. The sun was bright, but it was not so warm as it had been when he went inside, only its brightness seemed left to it. For years he had found comfort in knowing that if the sun were suddenly to go out its light would continue to reach the earth for eight minutes afterward, it had seemed a saving period of grace to him. But now he asked himself where the comfort lay, what if the sun were already out?" Coming full circle, the novella ends with a depiction of young people who have aged quickly in the rapid calculation of compromise registered and internalized, "breaking up into pairs and small groups to scatter themselves here and there . . . They walked through the night like old men and old women who have been through it all before. And he, not following them, looked up to greet the full moon overhead. It was an anemic stand-in for the sun, and cold, but at least a man could bear to look at it." With sentences as well-poised as anyone who has written English prose, and an almost unfathomable compassion for the least noticeable "slings and arrows" of modern life, Woolf's work remains a treasure to be relished, paid attention to and, now more than ever, brought back into wider circulation.

Henry Miller — Quiet Days in Clichy [1956]

G.N. FORESTER

Miller, Miller, hand on ball
Who's the most sexist of them all?

Henry Miller polarises. He has been described through the gamut of adjectives encompassing utterly scathing to gloriously idolising, not the least because of his blank disregard for publishing proprieties and reader sensibilities, which, depending on the end of the spectrum one chooses to sit, means he is either lauded or loathed.

He commences *Quiet Days in Clichy* with a spare prose, an insightful prose, at times even a euphonious prose, which, while interesting, valuable, and a self-inflicted necessary part of one's reading experience, fails to inspire a search for more of his works. One could say I've scratched my itch, we've had our fling, and Henry—it was nice knowing you but you were fated to be never more than the curious affair of the *dilettante* in the nighttime, another notch in my totem pole of writers to be savoured and not sainted.

Because for all the gems of wit, the wayward little asides, the rawness of emotion and the peering he affords inside his soul, Henry Miller re-scribing in his mid years this semi-autobiographical glimpse of a younger life in Paris as a destitute writer re-confirms and demonstrates a truly hideous objectification of women, of his muses, his lusts, his toys, his *objets du desir*, his vessels, his fucks-for-the-sake-of-fucking and nothing-to-do-with-art's-sake holes-in-one, when not in two. He reveals a terrible impoverishment of spirit in how he describes his slam-bangs and piss-insides. He simply doesn't see *members* of the opposite sex as anything other than tools for his own tool, grist for his mill, fodder to be cudded *ad infinitum*.

All true in stark, monochromatic form, until page eighty-one of *Quiet Days in Clichy*, when Miller is revealed in subtle, aquarelle tones and his story in deft, mostly gentle, even heart-rending, prose both assured and vivid, no longer a newspaper reporter's brutal rendition of action but a mature reflection of scene and character, thought and deed. The latter third of the book shows a sensitivity, an empathy, a willingness to understand himself in the context of women, rather than them in the context of himself; he admits even to that most treacherous and debilitating of emotions: love, consummated, forsaken, and finally, remorsefully, with the remembrance of too little, too late, eternally a promise of what might have been.

To call him misogynistic is as crudely misunderstanding of his attitude towards women as is labelling his work pornography. In the earlier part of *Quiet Days in Clichy* he indicates no hatred, no desire to abuse, demean or belittle, simply an inability to imagine or acknowledge the *personness* of women, the validity of their (and his own) feelings, all he can grasp is a reality in which women are not conceived as anything other than receptacles for his own *grace*, he is constrained to acknowledge them in relation to himself. Monstrously egotistical, but falling short of misogyny.

In the latter part of the book he eviscerates himself, he bleeds emotion, and in the sense of trailing after an illusion, women are a figure on a pedestal remaining forever beyond his reach; he has been enthralled, burned, made aware of the needs of the *other* and learned, by that experience, of the depth of his own. Women still represent a challenge, a trophy, an object to be acquired and enjoyed, but they are no longer mere *things*, puppets to be bought and traded on the whim of a moment, but forays within the vast unknown of the human soul, who can wreak havoc or dismiss him with the ease of flicking ash from a burning *Gauloises*.

Muriel Spark — The Comforters [1957]

KIM FAY

ART & OMISSION

As a reader, I choose novels for enrichment and entertainment. As a writer, I choose novels to learn craft. I read Graham Greene to learn how to develop psychological tension. I read Michael Ondaatje to learn how to weave poetry into plot. I read Penelope Lively to learn how to layer a story.

I read these writers and many others to learn how to add elements to my fiction.

Then there is Muriel Spark.

I read Spark to understand the art of omission.

If omitting equals trusting your readers, then Spark possesses absolute trust, because she often leaves out more than she includes in her spare, elegant, incisive, fanged fiction. What's most impressive to me is that this talent wasn't honed over the course of her career. She was a master of it in her very first novel.

Published in 1957 when Spark was 39, *The Comforters* is one of those fearless books that makes a writer sigh with admiration and envy.

To describe the plot is nearly impossible. Carolyn is a recent convert to Catholicism. She is also a writer working on a book called *Form in the Modern Novel*. When she begins to hear voices and the sound of a typewriter (The Typing Ghost), she fears that she might be a character in a novel that mirrors—or is being constructed by—her own life.

Adding to Carolyn's dramas is Laurence, who is in love with her, and whose grandmother might or might not be a diamond smuggler, as well as Baron Stock, a bookseller obsessed with the country's leading Satanist. All characters connect to one another (though you have to hang on tight to make some connections), even the side characters, whose quirkiness makes them ideal for a list of suspects in an Agatha Christie mystery. While Spark never overwrites, each of her characters, no matter how minor, feels fully formed due to her ability to capture the essence of a person in a mere sentence or so. This description of a religious busybody who harasses Carolyn is a perfect example:

"However, as soon as Mrs. Hogg stepped into her room, she disappeared, she simply disappeared. She had no private life whatsoever. God knows where she went in her privacy."

When Spark wrote *The Comforters*, she was a recent convert to Catholicism. This, and hallucinations she experienced while taking Dexedrine, influenced the creation of Carolyn. But many authors take their own experiences and weave them into stories. Spark is among the rare few who use this technique to lift their stories to a higher, universal level. Spark's scenes are rich fragments that the reader must piece together with her own assumptions, interpretations, and experiences to create a coherent narrative.

The Comforters is part parody, part satire, part love story, part mystery, part metafiction, part hyper-realism and part morality tale. That is the beautiful thing about Spark—she cannot be categorized. Her wonderful first novel is not my favorite (I am smitten with *The Girls of Slender Means*), but it is where I would tell readers to start. For a deeper understanding of the power of faith and art, I would tell them to read carefully, not what is on the page, but what isn't.

For unlike Spark's own Roman Catholicism, there is no such thing as a sin of omission in *The Comforters*.

Alexander Trocchi — Cain's Book [1960]

GILL TASKER

Alexander Trocchi's *Cain's Book* (1960) stays with you long after you stop reading. *Cain's Book* is narrated by Joe Necchi, arguably a fictional personae of Trocchi, who is writing his own 'Cain's Book'. Like Trocchi himself, Necchi was originally from Glasgow but had travelled to live in Paris in the early 1950s, before settling in New York City in the late 1950s. Necchi takes work as a scow captain, transporting waste in and around Manhattan's waterways, and although Necchi occasionally touches upon terra firma, the dislocated watery setting allows Necchi— a heroin addict—to consciously cultivate the stance of the outsider (the allusion to the outcast biblical figure Cain in the title similarly suggests this). Both high on heroin, and removed from civilisation on the scow, Necchi is doubly 'far out'. Indeed, Trocchi's treatment of addiction in the text is particularly striking: on the opening page, the protagonist unapologetically states 'Half an hour ago I gave myself a fix'.[1]

Cain's Book can be read as a novel, but it should perhaps be regarded as an 'anti-novel'. The novel rejects any sense of narrative arc, and instead, the reader is taken on an intensely intimate and wayward journey through time, place, and space, spanning Necchi's childhood in Glasgow, through to New York, whilst simultaneously plunging the reader into the depths of his deeply subjective and drugged consciousness. The non-linear structure of the narrative mirrors narcotic-induced drifting in and out of various states of mind without any apparent order or reason, and the writing process is also a theme that is explored; Necchi struggles to write his 'Cain's Book', and Trocchi uses his protagonist to raise questions about authorship, the creative process, aesthetics, and literature itself.

---

1 Alexander Trocchi, *Cain's Book*, (London: Calder, 1998; 1960), p. 9.

Heroin also impacts upon the text thematically, formally, and politically. Necchi is continually outspoken about what he calls the 'barbarous laws' in America, which restricts his—and other addicts'—existential freedom. As Necchi states, such 'hysterical attitudes' mean that the usual destination of the junkie is 'prison, madhouse, morgue'.[2] Thus, *Cain's Book* can be seen a text in which Trocchi, via Joe Necchi, critiques top-down authority and fights for rights and resistance. Moreover, the unconventional—even radical—last line of *Cain's Book* states that 'nothing is ending, and certainly not this'. With its absolute rejection of *telos*, this 'ending' was Trocchi's attempt to redefine literary practice, to subvert novelistic tradition, and to align literature more with life: Trocchi later stated in his sigma portfolio that these areas should 'no longer be divided'.[3]

Cain's Book is described by William S. Burroughs as 'a classic of addiction, like De Quincey'.[4] It is undoubtedly this, but as I hope I have implied here, it is also so much more.

---

2 Ibid., p. 13.
3 Alexander Trocchi, 'sigma: A Tactical Blueprint' in Andrew Murray Scott (ed.), *Invisible Insurrection of a Million Minds: A Trocchi Reader*, (Edinburgh: Polygon, 1991), p. 199.
4 William Burroughs interviewed in ibid., p. 163.

Michel Butor — Mobile [1962]

JOHN TREFRY

...CALL NUMBERS...
STUDY FOR A REPRESENTATION OF BUTOR'S *MOBILE*

Pitch dark... (3 A.M., solar time)... the blank page of a book beneath a lamp, the cone of light reflecting in the shuttered window. Dark pervades the blank grain; its song of eerie quavers prints through an open screen door. The text does not divest of seeping darkness. Paranoia that the book will never be found in the library is a time capsule concern. Books in libraries. Which brings our attention to the location of each book... *rioting deliriously through life like superimposed waterfalls, half rhythm, half darkness...* its singular magic, its singular sadness, the edition of *Jacques Roubaud's* THE GREAT FIRE OF LONDON blocked by a sprinkler pipe cannot be taken from the shelf... *to feel the delicious echo of the sun in the air of midnight...* Always a counterweight of darkness on the globe. The illusion of spaciousness in the dark. The obscure parallax of time's referents, the creeping exhumation of the public domain, what picture of the United States does it construct? *Thomas Jefferson* is buried beneath dismembered parts of *Francis Scott Fitzgerald*, beneath *Zane Grey*. For much the same reason, PAUL'S BOUTIQUE could not be produced today. The cautious glow of a tablet computer on a front porch. THE LIGHT OF THE WESTERN STARS. It is night. THE DESERT OF WHEAT, TALES OF LONELY TRAILS, K IN THE JUNGLE. Or, it is morning. Pitch dark... *The darkness has a different texture...* A cautious glow slithers about the text. The characters that use the most ink depend on the typeface, but would often be: M, Q, W, B.

*

... The novel is so huge, as if sketched across the whole sky ... words, words ... The very deep did rot ... the quaint world described by the book exists in no other real material but ink, and only this ink ... *some unknown and equivocal mass of plasticity, capable of changing at will to nebulous approximations of the solid, liquid, gaseous, or tenuously unparticled states ...* A clustered fog of placenames idles against the buckram terrain. "Hello, Michelle! What is the location of the book?" "What book?" "Where is the book located?" These are real places. Atop Mount Oread in eastern Kansas, in a study carrell beside a window installed inside an older window ... *N-Dawg was here 2.10.10. Jesus was here 12-25-0000* ... long stretches of nothing ... *Your feet are here, and your gaze is elsewhere* ... The swaddled synechdoches of *Vladimir Nabokov*'s United States, of *Michel Butor*'s United States, the United States of the European academic. Enamored with the sensation of vastness, but not its implications. A landscape is defined by its juxtaposition around the only few humans in existence. Some devices of vast intimacy: buzzing telephone in THE CASTLE, water-powered telephony in ADA, the ice-cream Pleiades of MOBILE. Each spot, each time, as it is written, as it is read, is the only time, the only spot that exists. *Franz Kafka*'s AMERIKA takes place in a book. THE NATURE THEATER OF OKLAHOMA. Unto These Hills ... *Under the glow of summer stars ... the family show too large for any screen ... there are almost no limits to it ...*

Robert Pinget — The Inquisitory [1962]

? ? ?

Do I intend to write this syllabus entry on Robert Pinget's novel-in-questions (where no question mark ever appears) entirely in questions? Did I even need to ask that question, seeing how your eyes immediately processed the interrogative gimmick of this entry from a cursory glance at the page? Why, you may be wondering, are the short pieces in this syllabus known as 'entries'? Isn't that rather clinical a term for the pageantry of erudition and insight on show in this third festschrift from Verbivoracious Press? Do you expect me to answer that, or any self-posed-to-an-invisible audience question? Why use the question gimmick when *The Inquisitory* consists of both questions and their answers? Why not? Why, you are wondering, has this piece not yet summarised the plot of this novel, nor made an attempt to position the novel within its *nouveau roman* milieu, nor provided a potted bio of the author? Why do you want to know, invisible reader? Do you perhaps nurture a sneaking suspicion (why do suspicions always *sneak*?) that a contributor or two might have bailed out the Syllabus, and that the editors are having to pick up the slack (why is slack always *picked up*?) with several improvisations based on easily imitable formal experiments of certain books? Is admitting this unprofessional, refreshingly candid and brave, pathetic, or a mixture of all three? Is this novel as entertaining as Gilbert Sorrentino's brilliant experiment *Gold Fools*, where a *Boys' Own*-type western novel is rewritten in the interrogative to hugely satisfying satirical effect? Is Padgett Powell's whimsical *The Interrogative Mood*, a novel that far outsold the Sorrentino and Pinget, and reduces the concept to a series of aimless semi-amusing surreal questions, an irritating plunder of the genius on show in these little-read books? Isn't my opinion apparent? Does Louis Bury, who also writes a section in questions in his collection *Exercises in Criticism: The Theory and Practice of Literary Constraint*, concur? Do you have any idea how addictive writing in this mood is? Do you think I should write a book-length study of these three novels to be written in questions (unless you discount this one, seeing as answers appear too)? Do you think I would waste my time on such a criminally narrow specialist area when there are more exciting crescents to be explored, such as a comprehensive study of the Scottish avant-garde scene? Is that, you say, some attempt to be knowing or smarmy? Do you think I would ever be flippant about literature? Are you trying to tarnish my reputation? What reputation? Now who's being smarmy? Do you think asking oneself questions while pretending to address them to an invisible audience is an insanity signifier? Should I eat the collected works of Pinget to prove I am sane? Do you think condiments are a wise idea? Shall I start in publication order, or in preference order? Do you think that this book I am holding in my left hand won't fit in my mouth without prior shredding or prior lubrication of the lips? What, did you really believe I would end this 'entry' on the phrase 'prior lubrication of the lips'?

B. S. Johnson — Omnibus [1964-1971]*

NICOLAS TREDELL

Johnson did not write for the person on the Clapham omnibus and was not omnibused in his lifetime; but the stops on the route of his posthumous charabanc are like those in many lives, and its origin and terminus—birth and death—are universal. Johnson's obsession with mortality may make readers reluctant to board his bus, like the man in the film *Dead of Night* who refuses to get on because he recognizes the conductor, with his cheerful 'room for one more inside, sir!', as the driver of a horsedrawn hearse in his dream. But Johnson's death-mask was Janus-faced, turned to both quick and dead. On the Johnson omnibus, in the midst of death, we are in life.

The journey starts with a portrait of the architect as a young man working as a supply teacher, a patronless Michelangelo reinscribed in twentieth-century London as Albert from the Angel in Islington, dubbed 'Albert Angelo' by one of his pupils (179). There is vivid mimesis in *Albert Angelo*, for instance in the brilliant pages that evoke our eponymous hero taking a lesson, with his words to his pupils in the left-hand column, his private thoughts on the right. But the cushions of realism were too comfortable for Johnson; he had to jolt his passengers; thus *Albert Angelo* disrupts its hitherto well-fashioned narrative with that 'almighty aposiopesis', 'OH, FUCK ALL THIS LYING!' (163, 167). But the verb is ambivalent; its angry rejection could also figure a covert desire to fuse with fiction, to penetrate and possess it.

We continue our journey with *Trawl*, but as in a dream, the mode of transport shifts to a ship, as the narrator goes to sea to 'trawl the delicate mesh of my mind over the snagged and broken floor of my past'

---

* B. S. Johnson, *Omnibus: Albert Angelo; Trawl; House Mother Normal* (London: Picador, 2004). Each novel in the omnibus edition retains its original setting and pagination.

(21). Autobiography in the form of a novel, but shaped like fiction and seduced by the siren lure of language into an eloquence that echoes Homer, as in this sunset: 'great blazing streamers bar the sky like long banners at a tourney, the light alchemizes the brass of the bridge into winedark gold' (43). And the end of *Trawl* brings the sailor home from the sea, hoping, like Odysseus, that the woman will be waiting.

The image of the tourney recurs ironically in *House Mother Normal*, where the elderly residents of the House Mother's anti-home fight wheelchair tourneys and play pass the parcel with turds. This is the last scene of all in Jaques Johnson's seven ages, but it is not quite sans everything. Vitality glows in the memories, fading coals, of the less amnesic residents and, though monstrously, in the House Mother herself, a priestess who claims that her acts protect the faith of the members of her flock who still believe: 'what would happen if they were to turn their disgust on God for taking away control over their own sphincter muscles [...]?' (197) Then, as the omnibus nears its terminus, the House Mother reveals herself as 'the puppet or concoction of a writer' (204), and the readers disembark, rattled and rejuvenated, into their own lives.

Nicolas Tredell: 28 Sept 2014

Raymond Queneau — The Blue Flowers [1965]

INEZ HEDGES

Queneau's world is one that you find yourself living in once you have encountered it. His fiercely joyful readers regularly meet to celebrate the "brouchtoucaille" or soup-pot supper that the inhabitants of the "ville natale", or native city of *Saint Glinglin*, consume on their annual holiday (the recipe varies, but the novel specifies that the pot is never washed out and last year's delicious remains are mixed into the new mush). At their regular conferences scholars and aficionados throw food, initiate one another into an ever growing number of "secret" societies, concoct strange machines that generate random poetry, and consume vast quantities of wine that bears the Queneau label. The erstwhile toastmaker of these feasts, André Blavier, reigned until his death over the Queneau archive in the small Belgian city of Verviers. He amassed photocopies of all the manuscripts and notes, as well as versions of the novels in over two dozen languages. Researchers could peruse such gems as the dream Queneau had of Lacan (who once belonged to the surrealist movement), and follow the evolving structure of each novel from the writer's copious notes. Queneau was also a mathematician, a practitioner of 'pataphysics, a member of the experimental Oulipo, the scribe of Kojève's lectures on Hegel, and a participant in any number of literary games—but as he admonishes from a flyer that Blavier once printed up, "Y a pas que la rigolade, y a l'art." ("It's not just about joking around, d'ya know, it's also about art").

Readers soon find that the novels color their perception of the real world. Isn't that French waiter Alfred from *Les Derniers jours* (The Last Days)—so perfect in his movements and so sure of his astrological charts that he is bound to win the lottery someday by playing the right number? Isn't that door with flaking paint in the Midi the mysterious one that opens to realms unknown in *Le Chiendent* (The Bark Tree)? Is my hapless friend not like Valentin Brû from *Le Dimanche de la vie* (The Sunday of Life), who goes on his honeymoon alone because his new wife has to mind the shop? You have entered a charmed circle. With Queneau your life will be more amusing, and your miseries more bearable because you will be able to smile at them.

Then there is the language. For English versions, we have the marvelous Barbara Wright. No one else compares with her when it comes to translating Queneau. Consider the transposed neologisms from *The Blue Flowers* (Les Fleurs bleues): "blagatory" and "screwpilating." Whenever the bargeman Cidrolin goes to sleep he becomes the Duc of Auge, galloping through the centuries on his talking horse until he reaches the French revolution; while the Duke dreams he is Cidrolin (Queneau loved the cinema, and this parallel editing, juxtaposing different time frames, is a film device *par excellence*). Strangely enough, both Cidrolin and the Duke have triplet daughters whom they have to marry off, and love to drink essence of fennel . . .

I encountered Queneau by chance, in a bookstore in Geneva after my wallet was pickpocketed in a Swiss bank. The book was *Les Fleurs bleues*. Thank you, gentle pickpocket, for this graceful note in my life.

Alan Burns — Celebrations [1967]

JOSEPH ANDREW DARLINGTON

Alan Burns' cut-up novel *Celebrations* (1967) is arguably the finest novel that a writer has produced using that technique. Burns made great use of experimental practices but his creations always transcended their origins; they became texts readable in themselves, beyond mere curiousities. Nine months after his death, I printed off all the internet had to say about this still underappreciated writer and cut it up. Consider it a celebration of his life, if you will ...

Alan was born in London, with ideas about
family. He told an Army ideas about
Service in the Royal Army Cubists with the
                              Anarchists with the
           Cries and rhythms.
Newspapers for libel. You want it or not?
Alan's early novels. Hitler knew it. And the
Later ones kicked out of Germany: "Nothing is
Too insecure as a new form of art".

The second of three sons of Harold and Annie, into a middle-class first published in 1967, Alan Burns employed his American interviewer. Major works include a warehouse by the Thames, and so on.

Became a barrister in 1956. Black and white keys in 1967, Alan Burroughs, makes use of such work for Reynolds News and researches their funny ideas about juxtaposing odd chronology, dreamlike Economics, and checked their funny ideas about the cut-technique.

1960s on, he has been associated with feelings.
Writers influenced by Rayner Heppenstall and a half. Perhaps Quin and its informal leader B.S. Johnseemed to have been allies as he worked on short film
                                        And B.S. Johnsee those…

Diverting, iconoclastic, and compulsively read; most exultant in my Burns queue. After the authors (as well as Burns himself): J.G. Ballard, Vietnam War, tough outlines of plot quite
John Hawkes, Tom Mallin, B.S. Johnsexploding tendency, weird non-narrative way.
and Alan Sillitoe   Er in *Celebrations*, so

Celebrations is where Williams is given one bliss; his two sons, a
                        pretty hard-
                      one with a
                          review of
                            the sentence and

it's selling for £75 plus posted 5 of 5 stars
Pretty special because
                Stars.
Alan Burns was perusable at my local uni library. I'm on it.
True vocation was writage. I wish I had the money, the fact that it's signed

Celebrations (1967) on the surface continued to
turn away from an exploitation of the sentence. You're
introduced to a group of men with sentence drives. One
employer and supervisor of herb is left uncertainly
early in the plot.

She put his hand out as *a* slipped its moorings.
        Wool dress with red Modernism and American Culture.

THE SYLLABUS

One is
      promptly factory. Williams, the father, is
as arranged. She and psychic-son Phillip died.

    "You don't need much.
Born yesterday, I've done all the things,
Had all the night life, not recently,
Now it doesn't interest me". She
      Quiet, dressed in black,
      Father was nearly seventy.
        He used to have
        been three storeys
        of soft. She was

      Machines,
        and

Alan Burns, who has died aged 83. *Celebrations*: the ritualised events labelled variously as experimental, surreal and avant garde, look at the rise and collapse of industrial
Joyce and his contemporaries. In years, familial details are perhaps of overriding significance
and B.S. Johnson.

Another vampire, family, mind
Literary and visual. I
    His collages. It was
    The pictures together
    Collages – a collage and plotting out
        Consciously searching for

God was God he said. How about we suffer through the experience of her moral comparisons just once, on the street.

Guillermo Cabrera Infante — Three Trapped Tigers [1967]

PABLO MEDINA

TTT: A CUBA OF THE MIND

Three Trapped Tigers, by the Cuban Guillermo Cabrera Infante, was the first truly Cuban novel I ever read. It begins with a monologue by the emcee of Tropicana, the most luxurious nightclub in pre-revolutionary Havana:

Showtime! Señoras y señores. *Ladies and gentlemen. Muy* buenas noches, damas y caballeros, tengan todos ustedes. *Good-evening, ladies and gentlemen.* Tropicana, el cabaret MÁS fabuloso del mundo… 'Tropicana' *the most famous night-club in the WORLD… presenta… presents…*

It was the winter of 1968 in the Bronx when a friend presented me with a copy of novel. The Spanish title *Tres tristes tigres*, or *Three Sad Tigers*, is derived from a Spanish *trabalenguas*, or tongue-twister, that the English title couldn't possibly evoke. Tongues twist differently in different languages, depending on their sounds. Nevertheless, it's a good substitute. The three heavily stressed initial beats make it a drum roll, a hammer hammering (in the morning, in the evening). The English does something else the Spanish doesn't do. It directs us to the questions that bloop out of the rolling wave of the narrative: Who are those tigers? Where are they trapped? And how? Those questions are not, thankfully, answered in the text, or are themselves their own answers. The three principal characters are three variations of the narrator's personality. As the book moves through the city of Havana, they split open like pink, sweet papayas and what comes out is language and more language, love juice at first sight.

The author asserts in a note at the beginning of the Spanish edition "that the book is written in Cuban. That is, written in the different dialects of Spanish spoken in Cuba and the writing is nothing more than an attempt to capture the human voice in midflight." They say Cabrera Infante is the Cuban Joyce. I say he's the Cuban Mark Twain. Correction: he's Mark Twain disguised as James Joyce writing in Spanish.

At the time I received this gift of all gifts, I was trying to unravel the skein of the many threads of New York English in order to find my voice, my tongue, which was and would always remain Cuban, disguised now, of necessity, in the words of New World Anglo urban speech. Imagine my discovery that language flies, that it can be captured, that it is multiple and various and new, all fallacy of mastering it aside.

I carried the book like a talisman that winter of my discontent and read in the bathroom, on the subway, in English class. "What is that you're reading, Medina?" "A book about Havana by a Cuban writer, Father." "Keeping up with your Spanish, are you?" I said yes, and he approved. I didn't tell him I was keeping up with New York, that Havana of the world; with sex, the Holy Grail of adolescence; and with Cuba and the night (or are they one and the same? as José Martí once asked, writing from New York).

Over the years I wore the pages down. The spine cracked, the cover fell apart. The friend who gave me *Three Trapped Tigers* died of AIDS. I replaced the old copy with a new hardcover edition, which lies on my desk alongside the English version by Donald Garner and Suzanne Jill Levine. I couldn't replace my friend, but he sits high on my list of benefactors, just below Cabrera Infante, the author of this crazy, fractured, explosive, salacious, and oh so very Cuban book that taught me how to ride the wave, taught me how to write.

Macedonio Fernández — The Museum of Eterna's Novel [1967]

STEVE PENKEVICH

THE FIRST GOOD ESSAY

'He who imagines will never know non-being.'

The essayist should begin with a quote, as above, from the novel to be discussed, in this case Macedonio Fernández's exquisitely exploratory *The Museum of Eterna's Novel*. This is a good start. The reader will feel invited to consider the implications of the quote choice, and the essay can then continue with both essayist and reader introduced to one another through this handshake of consciousness. The essayist should mention that Fernández was a mentor of sorts to Jorge Luis Borges, as this pairing invokes thoughts of Borges's literary career exploring metaphysics. With the tone set, the essayist may proceed to a discussion of the book.

First, address the mechanics of the novel, such as the fifty-some prologues that proceed the 'novel' portion of the book. Discuss how dedicating the novel to the 'skip-around-reader' highlights his unconventional and convoluted style. The essayist is advised to provide a quote that examines the style and elucidates the importance of creating art:

> *'he who reads only seeking the final resolution is seeking what art should not provide, his interest is in the merely vital, not in a state of consciousness: the only artistic reader is the one who does not seek resolution.'*

It is key for the essayist to investigate how this novel focuses on the mechanics of a book and not plot, the engine and not the motion.

The essayist must elucidate on the characters, perhaps as below:

Fernández discusses the creation process of characters and the restraints on an author in creating them, such as how it would require a genius to be able to aptly create a 'genius character'. His characters are constantly making demands of their author, most prominently his inability to give them actual life. We all need a room of one's own, and within *Museum* Fernández attempts to provide as such for reader, author, and characters alike in the metaphysical realm of La Novela. The state of Being is forever under the looming shadow of non-being, however, Fernández posits that we cheat non-being through the act of creation. Through creating art we become Creator characters, enhance our metaphysical space and experience *'the birth pangs'* of life. Art gives us immortality.

Finally, the essayist should summarize the intentions on the novel, hopefully with use of a quote.

> *'I thus leave a perfect theory of the novel, an imperfect execution thereof, and a perfect plan for its future execution.'*

Explain how Fernández wants readers to take what they have learned in order to further the advancement of literature. Also, point out that Fernández says of critics: *'all you really know is what Perfection is not.'* Explore how *Museum* serves as a metaphysical tool-kit for creating art.

Conclude as such: While *Museum*, with its ponderousness and obfuscating structure may not be what critics may call the 'perfect novel', it is indeed an essential tool-kit to utilize and strive towards perfection.

Anna Kavan — Ice [1967]

KRISTINE RABBERMAN

In the opening paragraphs of Anna Kavan's *Ice*, the narrator notes, "Reality had always been something of an unknown quantity to me. At times this could be disturbing. Now, for instance." With these ominous words, Kavan ushers in a dreamscape—cold, fragmented, unrelenting. In shimmering prose, she paints a vision of the deadly beauty of a world that is becoming encased in ice, in which the man-made horrors of wars, cruelty, and deceit pale in the face of nature's greater power:

> Cold coruscations of rainbow fire pulsed overhead, shot through by shafts of pure incandescence thrown out by mountains of solid ice towering all round. Closer, the trees round the house, sheathed in ice, dripped and sparkled with weird prismatic jewels, reflecting the vivid changing cascades above. Instead of the familiar night sky, the aurora borealis formed a blazing, vibrating roof of intense cold and colour, beneath which the earth was trapped with all its inhabitants, walled in by those impassable glittering ice-cliffs. The world had become an arctic prison from which no escape was possible, all its creatures trapped as securely as were the trees, already lifeless inside their deadly resplendent armour.

Three characters reappear throughout the novel: the nameless narrator, who has served as a soldier and as an adventurer in tropical climes; the warden, whose power often is reflected in his control over scores of armed men; and a painfully slender woman, whose silvery hair and dark eyes mark her as otherworldly. The woman is damaged, reflecting the horror of abuses first suffered in childhood and continued in adulthood. These characters appear and reappear throughout *Ice*, as the narrator searches for the woman, who sometimes eludes his grasp, sometimes is a prisoner of the warden, and sometimes, briefly, is caught by the narrator, only to be lost to him again. The cruelty, longing, and fear embodied in their entangled relationships play out against a stark backdrop of war and treachery—and all the time, the ice is bearing down on them inexorably.

Creating a sense of dislocation in *Ice*, transitions throughout are abrupt, throwing the reader from present to past to vision to dream and back again. Reading this novel is like being trapped in a labyrinthine nightmare, with no clear sense of what is real and what is memory or illusion. Kavan uses these abrupt shifts in perspective or setting almost as if she were fast-forwarding a film. Her readers are disoriented by these rapid changes, only to be anchored again as they catch a glimpse of a familiar figure—the silver-haired woman in a gray overcoat, the warden peering out of the shadows, a shadowy army of bodyguards, a ship's captain offering a means for pursuit or flight. Kavan eerily creates a claustrophobic world, in which characters seem destined to play out the same actions endlessly, with no hope for escape or forgiveness. The central mystery in *Ice* is whether the narrator and the woman will break free of old patterns of pain, cruelty, and loss before the ice consumes them.

J.M.G. Le Clézio — Terra Amata [1967]

KEITH MOSER

RECOUNTING THE UNIVERSAL SAGA OF EXISTENCE

Published in 1967 by Gallimard, J.M.G. Le Clézio's novel *Terra Amata* has been relatively forgotten by critics in comparison to his more well-known canonical works of fiction such as *Le Procès-verbal*, *Désert*, and *Le Chercheur d'or*. This experimental text, seamlessly blending literary genres and transgressing disciplinary boundaries, is clearly reminiscent of the *Nouveau Roman* movement. Nonetheless, regardless of this undeniable influence, this early narrative is one of the most highly original, thought provoking, and innovative works that the 2008 Nobel Laureate in Literature has ever written. This often neglected novel from the first half of the author's illustrious career is undoubtedly overdue for recognition.

In *Terra Amata*, in addition to mixing poetry and prose, Le Clézio incorporates drawings. The varied nature of the prose immediately strikes the reader. The writer amalgamates lyrical passages, so poetic that these should really be read aloud, with creative and sometimes hermetic sections in which he probes the limitations of language itself and compels the reader to take an active role in the creation of meaning. In this vein, the chapters entitled "Saying incomprehensible words" and "asking indiscreet questions" are of particular interest.

In spite of the aforementioned experimentation and wordplay, which likely explains why this work has failed to resonate with much of the general public, *Terra Amata* is one of the most profound novels, from a philosophical perspective, that Le Clézio has ever published. In this ambitious literary project, the reader follows the adventures of the protagonist Chancelade from birth to death. As the author will later directly confess in one of the many metafictional sections of the narrative, Chancelade is a metaphor for the human condition. In this early text, the protagonist's searing ontological pain is counterpointed by an equally poignant *joie de vivre* that beckons him to taste, touch, smell, see, and hear everything that life affords. Similar to the sensual material ecstasy articulated by the Camusian narrator of *Nuptials*, *Terra Amata* represents a deep valorization of human life despite the evident mortality that is inscribed in the genetic code of every *homo sapien* that has ever roamed this planet.

Finally, *Terra Amata* not only chronicles the various stages of human life, but it also recounts the universal story of existence in all of its divergent forms. Delving within the principles of modern science, Le Clézio endeavors to portray a small glimpse of what it means for a sentient being to be tossed in the chaos of existence arbitrarily by indifferent cosmic forces that predate our species by billions of years. In an interconnected and interdependent biosphere randomly recycling energy and material particles to continue impersonal organic cycles originally set in motion by a "big bang" approximately four and half billion years ago, Chancelade strives to find his small place in the greater cosmic whole that sustains all abundant life on this planet where we live and die. In short, *Terra Amata* is a must-read because it offers a cogent and scientifically accurate description of the most tragic and beautiful saga ever told: existence.

Flann O'Brien — The Third Policeman [1967]

ALEX JOHNSTON

A promising initiate in the halls of learning is granted access to obscure codices. He acquires knowledge through a hole in his face. It drives him mad. However, he doesn't realise it. He thinks he's just smart. He assumes the mask of class joker, but the knowledge within him is incubating into something else.

He produces a book: a clever but desultory jeux d'esprit, which earns him the approval of distinguished elders. He's content to have arrived. It's all been a doddle. What he doesn't realise is that that first book was only a rustling in the shirtfront of a functionary.

When *The Third Policeman* burst out of Brian O'Nolan's chest at his family dinner table over the course of 1939 and 1940, he must have been as unnerved as the crew of the Nostromo in *Alien*, watching that penile chicken spring from the chest cavity of their hapless executive officer. *The Third Policeman* was written in the immediate aftermath of the Irish Counter-Revolution. The 1937 Constitution of Ireland had enshrined the Catholic church at the centre of national life and relegated women to the status of second-class citizens, causing indescribable misery in Irish life for the next seven decades and beyond. O'Nolan, who went straight from college into the Irish civil service, was part of the process by which the new state consolidated itself. He was a loyal company man but his unconscious, which with all other manifestations of cosmopolitan quackerdoodle he was so quick to laugh off, spoke for something or someone else.

The Third Policeman has been claimed as a queer text, but its power and menace come from its dread of its own queerness. The women characters are inconspicuous drudges; the only physical intimacy that the men desire is with bicycles. (Remember that the phrase 'village bike' is an insulting term for a promiscuous woman.) O'Nolan claimed that the only good thing about the book was the plot, but the plot is a pretext for its mood: a combination of reverence for nature, terror of authority and warped tenderness.

We know this mood. We're more at home with it than Brian O'Nolan was. In *Alien*, it's in the android Ash's description of the alien: 'I admire its purity. A survivor . . . unclouded by conscience, remorse, or delusions of morality.' The policemen's pleasures are celibate and masturbatory. MacCruiskeen makes music on instruments only he can hear, and crafts artifacts that only he can perceive. Sergeant Pluck's notion of law is that it's a way of justifying what he wants to do anyway. Frustrated because the narrator, being nameless, isn't anyone, and therefore can't be prosecuted, he reasons that since the narrator is nobody, his death would amount to nothing more than 'an insanitary abstraction in the backyard' and is therefore fine.

O'Nolan survived the creation of *The Third Policeman* only by isolating it from the public. After his publishers rejected it, he left the manuscript on the sideboard and stumbled on, recycling its least interesting elements, the De Selby stuff, into 1964's flatulent *The Dalkey Archive*, the kind of book a zombie might have written. *The Third Policeman* remains his masterpiece: a perfect tragicomic nightmare of the sexual imagination of 20th century Ireland.

Ishmael Reed — *The Freelance Pallbearers* [1967]

JOSEPH McGRATH

Power: like anything, when looked at too closely it becomes absurd, so Power profits from any distance between the particular and the macro. Ishmael Reed's *The Freelance Pallbearers* is a flamboyant amplification and magnification of Power's peculiar particulars, boosted to such outrageous exaggeration that it creates its own alternative cartoon universe, although within it dreams of this one occasionally intrude.

It's a Nixonesque era seen through Bootsy Collins' oversized sunglasses enjoying whatever George Clinton was on (Reed was literary P-Funk before there *was* P-Funk), cutting a sharp and showy break from the grim realism of African-American literary tradition. *Freelance* is a wild silly riff on Ralph Ellison's *Invisible Man*, told in a brash pastiche of verbal styles ranging from street slang to pretentious Formal Standard English, the vacant come-ons of advertising to the quasi-philosophical contortions of a deeply conflicted religion.

Absurd Dickensification of names is usually associated with Thomas Pynchon, whose more bizarre monikers appear *after* the antics of *Freelance*'s Bukka Doopeyduk, Georgia Nosetrouble, U2 Polyglot, the Reverend Éclair Porkchop, as well as a next-door couple who lost their names in a lottery so go by M/neighbor and F/neighbor.

These folks get up to some seriously surreal racket in this romp through the hard-times travails imposed by big business, big medicine, big government, big religion, and big mouths everywhere shouting in deep funk dialect, often in big-letter caps: "KEEP IT UP YOU FREE-LOADEN COMMUNIST TAFFYPANTS SISSIES!"

Meanwhile, up above, Bukka's beloved ailing theocratic President reigns from the loo of an island motel, surrounded by dangerous black waters populated with hazards like " . . . extrasensory plants. (And believe you me, dem plants is hongry . . .)" where a crisis brews.

Our hero Bukka is a passive yes-man trying to get by, enduring all manner of indignity at work and at home where his new wife comes across as such an awful henpecking no-cleaning back-talking back-to-mama-runnin' stereotype that it becomes unclear whether this is our slow earnest conservative Bukka's perspective, a layered ironic parody of the trope, or just old-fashioned sexist humor aging badly.

Big Medicine is his first employment scene as a lower-order laborer charged with preparing patients for procedures left disturbingly vague, rendered as both privileged prerogatives and mightily unpleasant. He stumbles into his next gig as an actor in a ludicrously outré performance art outfit through which he's accidentally given an image makeover: as a radical agitator against everything he's ever held true.

The ensuing attention paradoxically draws him into the social orbit revolving around the island motel toilet seat of power. Micro Bukka goes macro, then his co-optation goes apocalyptic, exploding in a carnivalesque kaleidoscope of decadence so dense with references it's like decades of minor and mass media compressed into a clip show.

While a good bit of the weirdness seems very much of its time—some because it seems even weirder now, some because it *doesn't*—unintentionally amusing like the outfits our parents once wore, what gives this book legs is its brazen originality. You'll read nothing else like it.

Christine Brooke-Rose — Between [1968]

KATARZYNA BARTOSZYŃSKA

It's amazing how much you can understand when someone is speaking a language you don't know. Or, in the case of this book, ten or twenty languages (among them English, French, German, Turkish, Polish, Greek, Romanian, Danish, Italian, Dutch, Hungarian, and Czech.). *Between* is a kind of experiment in multilingual mood, a sinuous braid of tongues, with strands folding under and resurfacing. The plot, inasmuch as there is one, seems rather beside the point, though the various musings gesture towards certain lines of thought: history (both ancient and recent), borders, love, the body, the self. There is, or seems to be, a central character, a middle-aged woman who drifts across continents, waking up in hotel rooms that are all different but not really, to the sounds of a chambermaid or concierge offering variations on the same greeting. She is a translator, working at a political conference, and there is a romance, or perhaps a failed one, stilted conversations and misunderstandings. Unlike other multilingual works such as Gloria Anzaldua's *Borderlands*, the aim of actually using all the different languages in this book seems to be intended less as the authentic expression of a multicultural individual than as an effort to capture the sounds of a multilingual universe. How different are languages from each other, really? How is it that I recognize given phrases of this book as Romanian, and know what they are saying, despite never having learned the language or been to the place? Although the literature and cinema of travel so often focuses on feelings of alienation or estrangement, when one arrives in a foreign city there is also typically a delighted process of recognition, as words begin to map onto their referents and the intrepid explorer starts to piece together the meanings of frequently encountered phrases.

It is possible that one needs to have experienced the vertigo of extensive travel to properly appreciate this book. The strange placelessness of airplanes, their hushed voices, dim lighting, minute differences in a general template. It is further possible—even likely—that one must be at least somewhat multilingual to derive the full benefits of the work. Not so that one could know all of the languages used (you'd be hard-pressed to find a reader that did), but to know what it's like to shift between worlds, selves, parts of your life, so that you can enjoy the exhilarating feeling this book gives you of stimulating each of those parts in turn, drawing them out and weaving them together, traversing the gaps without entirely suturing them. A word will be repeated five times in as many different languages, as if to see which one is best suited, or whether they really are all the same, and of course they are not, and yet, and yet. Though it would seem that this is the kind of book one appreciates primarily in an abstract sort of way (admiring the idea, intending to read it but never quite wanting to), the experience of it is a pleasurable, rhythmic sort of hum, an enjoyment of the way the words fill your mind's mouth and reshape the tongue. The reader floats in a tranquil middling, both active and passive, sometimes merely hearing (or rather, seeing), sometimes understanding, sometimes in one language, sometimes in another: between.

Anthony Earnshaw and Eric Thacker — Musrum [1968]

KENNETH COX

Musrum is a book, of that much we can be certain, but who or what is its eponymous hero? Is Musrum a man or a mouse, a criminal or a creator, or a space in which to dream? Is Musrum an attic, a corner, an exit or a cellar? Is Musrum a ventriloquist's dummy, as his parrot believes, or is he none other than his double, Palfreyman? We *do* know that Musrum is terribly afraid of sponge cats ...

As the myth takes shape, with lucidity and internal coherence, like an eccentric fairytale, we learn that Musrum is some sort of demi-god who reigns from an Iron Castle in the land of Interstol and that his prized possession, a veritable Tree of Life in the form of a gigantic mushroom, is coveted by his adversary, the Weedking. The Tree is stolen from Musrum's garden by the Weedking, which leads to a convoluted military campaign—the Second Crimean War, no less, with a cast including gypsies and wolves—and the eventual resolution of this mock-Manichean struggle.

The result of a collaboration between a surrealist artist and a Methodist minister, Anthony Earnshaw and Eric Thacker, and published, much to their surprise, by Jonathan Cape in 1968, *Musrum* is a book very much outside of literature, a 'surrealist story' (Thacker) mixing narrative with aphorisms, axioms, inventories, drawings, maps and diagrams, creating a truly distinctive interaction of the verbal and visual. Humour, often absurdist and pun-rich, runs riotously throughout, with shifting meanings and wild paradoxes. However, this was not intended as some sort of avant-gardist literary-artistic experimentation. Far from it, this is a book that pulses with playful interchange, between kindred spirits who shared an impish contempt for the humdrum of reality, including literature, playfully re-inventing and re-arranging this reality in their common cause.

Earnshaw and Thacker, both in their mid-forties when *Musrum* was written (though 'written' seems a wholly inadequate term), had been close friends since their teens, and had long shared passions for surrealism, anarchism and jazz (think *Perdido Street Blues* by The New Orleans Wanderers), as well as drifting through the streets of their native Leeds, at that time a grimy, industrial city. Growing from an exchange of letters, *Musrum* was principally created for their own non-conformist pleasure and amusement, inventing a new world—reflected, inverted, topsy-turvy; defying conventional logic, gravity, mechanics, architecture, perspective, history and geography. The 'musroid' world is built from the attic downwards into thin air, starting at the top, level by level, thereby creating a myriad of other realities, multiplying and running amok in the imagination. A world where a window retains its view, no matter to which room it is transported. A world where bandits, to avoid recognition, rather than conceal their faces, blindfold their own eyes. A world like no other in a book that cannot be contained or categorised.

Find it, read it and its spores will seep into your dreams.

Nicholas Mosley — Impossible Object [1968]

SHIVA RAHBARAN

Freedom implies discoverable meaning in an act — Frederick Turner

The individual, and groupings of people, have to learn that they cannot reform society in reality, nor deal with others as reasonable people, unless the individual has learned to locate and allow for the various patterns of coercive institutions, formal and also informal, which rule him. No matter what his reason says, he will always relapse into obedience to this coercive agency while its pattern is with him. — Idries Shahj

Nicholas Mosley, one of the most prolific exploratory novelists of our time, admits that all his novels have always been concerned with one theme only: freedom. His novels could thus be seen as chapters of a single novel in which a single theme evolves: the possibility of man's freedom through overcoming the paradox of freedom. The paradox—or, as Mosley often calls it, the 'impossibility'—of freedom arises due to man's awareness of the necessity of limiting structures for freedom. Hence the question is: how could man fulfil the paradoxical task of overcoming these structures in order to attain freedom?

Each phase of his writing career dramatises one aspect of this endeavour which consequently leads onto the next phase and supersedes the previous one by addressing the possibility of overcoming the paradox of freedom on a higher level and in a more complex context. The existentialist, 'Sartrean' novels of a restless young soldier returning home from WWII are followed by writings of a man who finds meaning and freedom in Anglo-Catholic Christianity. These are in turn superseded by highly exploratory novels—*Accident* (1966); *Impossible Object* (1968)—that both depict the paradox of freedom and try to resolve it through the aesthetic observation of this paradox. For Mosley an 'Impossible Object' is thus both the embodiment of paradox and the overcoming of paradox: "*something impossible, like a staircase climbing a spiral to come out where it started or a cube with a vertical line at the back overlapping a horizontal one in front. These cannot exist in three dimensions but can be drawn in two; by cutting out one dimension a fourth is created.* **The object is that life is impossible;** *one cuts out fabrication and creates reality.*"*

In his following 'scientific phase', Mosley incorporates the views of scientists such as Gregory Bateson, Fritjof Capra and R. D. Laing, in order to show that humans are not at the 'mercy' of their genes, body, and brain, and can overcome the determining structures and workings of these, only if they learnt to 'watch' and 'allow' for them from a higher level of observation. From here it was only a matter of course that Mosley—up to the present day—became interested in the highest place of observation; namely, the Eye of God. In the subsequent phase of his novels he explores the mystical traditions—such as Taoism, Sufism, Gnosticism and Agnosticism—within major religions that try to lift humans to a higher level of being and *seeing*. It is only in this sphere that humans could find the possibility of *living* freedom.

---

* Mosley (*IO*), p218; original italics; my emphasis.

Vladimir Nabokov — Ada or Ardor [1969]

ROB FRIEL

Reading *Ada* for me was, at first, an act of spite—which, all things considered, is probably appropriate.

It was the spring of 2011 and I had just emerged from a winter-long funk, moved house, and started reading again. The sun was out and I felt myself coming back to the world—the people, the books—I had left behind during that long winter. Hermetic, self-absorbed isolation was no longer my game. The world had other beings in it again.

And so I found myself reflecting with frustration on Vladimir Nabokov, an author I had initially loved—until I read *Lolita* at age 18 I had never felt that "literature", in the highfalutin' and highly-stylized sense, was a thing that resonated in my bones—and found progressively more and more disappointing. *Pale Fire* was, yes, very clever, but its convolutions were wrapped around an ultimately simple and banal story about a cartoon madman, mistaken only on matters of trivial fact. What was there to chew on here? Reading Nabokov's own nonfiction writing gave me the chilly sense that he aimed, asymptotically, for a *pure lack of chewiness*: patterned cleverness for its own sake, human interest a worthless husk surrounding the combinational fruit, *Madame Bovary* a masterwork for the way it made artsy latticework out of the lives of people Flaubert uncomplicatedly despised.

Waving my anti-hermetic-self-absorption banner, I decided to make a clean break with Nabokov by reading what was, by most accounts, his most hermetic and least satisfying work. *Ada* reflected "the meltdown of artistic self-possession," wrote Martin Amis (Nabokov Big-Name Fan extraordinaire). It was long, obscure, wore down the patience even of acolytes. It took place on an imaginary planet. It was about *incest*, for

Chrissake. I was sure it would be the Master at his most self-absorbed. I was ready to stand at the heart of his inner sanctum, declare "no, this isn't enough", and stride off, head held high.

And so what did I make of *Ada*? At first, I couldn't believe my eyes. It was everything I had expected and more: Nabokovian self-indulgence unfolded without shame, coiling literary references grown gracelessly and kudzu-like across every page, smug cultured protagonists showing up straw man adversaries with no earthly counterbalance in sight . . .

And yet there was something there even at the start, a feeling of climbing a ladder into the past and upward into abstraction, back to something at once primal and unimaginably complicated, the mystical behind the everyday—a feeling that followed me through that whole blissful, sun-drenched summer. And then I finished Part 1.

Ada, if you stay with it, is a book that pulls the floor out from under you so many times that floor-pulling becomes a kind of continuous equilibrium state. It is not, as I initially thought, a solipsistic book with "no earthly counterbalance" to its own ego—it is rather a faux-solipsistic book that provides endless earthly counterbalances, but only implicitly. It is a finely-wrought edifice full of holes through which one glimpses endless possibilities, most of them bleak, and all of them running against the solipsistic grain. It is a (strangely) successful romantic novel, containing some of the best swoony prose I've ever read, that undermines and parodies its central romance in manifold ways. It is a 600-page paean to nostalgia that turns back on itself and becomes an indictment of the excesses of nostalgia. It is the perfect ironic novel, playing itself straight and undermining itself at once. The Master's inner sanctum turns out to be an *outer* sanctum as well.

Self-congratulation, solipsism, nostalgia, density, opacity—these materials harden into a ladder leading to some sunny and mystic realm of Forms where one can feel reality's polyvalent wind on one's neck. Nabokov turns inward and finds the whole universe, only in negative. Read *Ada*. Even if you don't like Nabokov; even if you *hate* Nabokov. There is time enough in your life to try climbing the ladder and see what you find at the top.

J.G. Ballard — The Atrocity Exhibition [1970]

RICK McGRATH

Programming the Psychodrill: Coded Sleep and Intertime. Dr Nathan lit his gold-tipped cigarette and studied the documents on the table. These were: (1) a ticket, good for admission on November 15, 1956, to the *This is Tomorrow* Pop Art exhibition in the Whitechapel Art Gallery; (2) electroencephalogram of Sigmund Freud; (3) black and white postcard of three people on a damaged overpass, identified on the reverse as Kline, Coma, and Xero; (4) diagram of a replicated and condensed metaphase eukaryotic chromosome; (5) five double-page magazine spreads of apparently unrelated headlines, type, and charts, dated 1958, identified only as *Project for a New Novel*. Dr Nathan looked up. "And you say these constitute an Atrocity Exhibition?"

Beach Fatigue. Traven wondered why he had so much freedom as he explored *The Terminal Beach* of Eniwetok in March, 1964. He looked around the pages of his story. Yes, his actions were dictated by his obsessions, but there was something else . . . what was new? What allowed him to ignore so many of the elements of continuity? There they were: *Subheads*. Infiltrators from ads and magazines, they tempt the reader on with conceptual clues. They also condense time. Individualize the texts. Traven also noticed how this artificial fragmentation gave the omnipotent narrator an opportunity to insert a mindscape of associative information from nearby tangents.

A History of Nothing. Ballard: "My original idea for *The Atrocity Exhibition* was that I would do collage illustrations . . . I originally wanted a large-format book . . . in which I could prepare the artwork—a lot of collages, material taken from medical documents and medical photographs, crashing cars and all that sort of iconography." This idea was rejected—too expensive to produce (and what about all that sex?)—but no matter, Ballard had already written all the *Atrocity* stories 1966-69, blending the ersatz science, characters, and headlines of *Project for a New Novel* with the subheads, intrusions, ersatz science and psychotic pilot from *The Terminal Beach* . . . and baking all the little cupcakes of copy in a hot oven of cold emotions. Without Ballard's illustrations, *The Atrocity Exhibition* is a warped spacetime collage of texts, an exhibition of fragmentary scenes in a gallery of free associations . . . in itself a grasp at a new kind of form—a 2D kit of 3D writing. One of the side effects is reader fatigue. Don't worry, the story is mostly present, but disguised as ADD. Or it might be a badly-edited late night *foreign* movie with many very odd commercials. Segue: what would *The Atrocity Exhibition* have been like if Ballard had published it as an art book? Our only clues are the five "Advertiser's Announcements" Ballard made 1967-71 and published in *Ambit* (my homage opposite), using the design of full bleed photo and overlying header and text—something he might have used in the illustrated book. As in *Atrocity*, there is deep fragmentation in these ads—the image and text bear only a conceptual relationship with each other—as if preparing us for the channel-jumping, flickering TV-image structure of the book.

Landscapes of the Dream. No one reads *The Atrocity Exhibition*—they imagine it.

Photo: Rick McGrath

Advertiser's Announcement

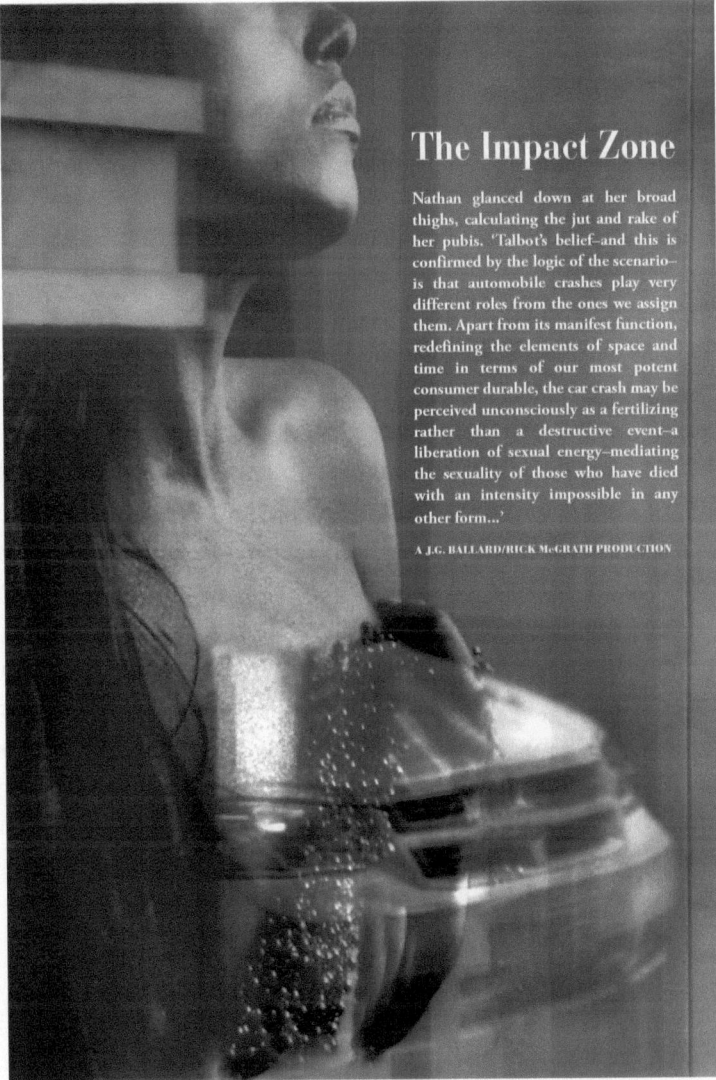

The Impact Zone

Nathan glanced down at her broad thighs, calculating the jut and rake of her pubis. 'Talbot's belief—and this is confirmed by the logic of the scenario—is that automobile crashes play very different roles from the ones we assign them. Apart from its manifest function, redefining the elements of space and time in terms of our most potent consumer durable, the car crash may be perceived unconsciously as a fertilizing rather than a destructive event—a liberation of sexual energy—mediating the sexuality of those who have died with an intensity impossible in any other form...'

A J.G. BALLARD/RICK McGRATH PRODUCTION

Pierre Guyotat — Eden Eden Eden [1970]

PETER BLUNDELL

Wyndham Lewis' BLAST manifesto, Allen Ginsberg's *Howl*, Samuel Beckett's *Not I* and even James Joyce's soliloquy of Mrs Bloom in Ulysses offer radical linguistic outpourings, with capital letters of affirmation, desire for freedom and expression and resounding YES at the finale. However, French writer Pierre Guyotat in his 1970 novel *Eden Eden Eden* within, mostly lower-case lines set apart by semi-colons—affords no such epiphanies despite its title's triple-appeal for paradise.

The epiphany for the intrepid reader here comes in the liberation of Guyotat's prose. The ability of his words almost free of context and character to throw us head-first into an experience that we couldn't possibly bare but still intimately share because we are of flesh and blood too and to further sustain this momentum for, in my English translation, 162 pages in one continuous sentence.

Eden recounts in seemingly real-time the semi-conscious adventures of Wazzag: a male prostitute who plies his trade for soldiers passing through desecrated war zones in the North African desert. He barely survives through episode after unrelenting episode of humiliating sex and casual violence. The book is no exploitation horror though, the graphic sex and brutal violence on each page are attack on literary language itself and a testing of the limits to write from the body that unsurprisingly was dimly-regarded by the French censor on publication who banned it.

The transgressive literary tradition that Guyotat is part of Genet, Bataille, and de Sade before them is clear but I like to consider this text in the same head to ear to eye space as Peter Brotzmann's free-jazz mammoth *Machine Gun* from 1968 and Shinya Tsukamoto's cyber-punk 1989 video nightmare *Tetsuo: The Iron Man*. Guyotat strips back his narrative to reveal only the most extreme sensations. There is no respite in form, context or establishing scene, neither segue or transition from one moment to the next: just a relentless catalogue of incidents in an all-consuming NOW! Brotzmann's army of horns similarly blast, erupt and ejaculate like said automatic weapon without any warning whilst Tetsuo's body under constant stress grows machine-like prosthetics losing human control in the process.

Despite coming thick and fast like a jackhammer I discovered a world in *Eden*. A world that opens in slow motion after fifty plus pages. As a reader I found I was only able to inhabit this world in a decelerated zone—cognitively against the speed of the action described. Whole sections read like treacle on sandpaper. Where the tiniest details buried in the text referring to the space the character resides in and moves into are subtly illuminated. An interior detail will indicate a ceiling above or light from nearby window, towards a point where there is now dirt beneath feet and sand blown in the face. The analogy comes to mind is time-lapse photography; where piecing one reading image to another forms the movement in the text. It is also writing that takes the scenic route around your anatomy, so the change is all over before reaching your head.

Raymond Federman — *Double or Nothing* [1971]

LANCE OLSEN

saturn's knowledge

"I like to remind myself the rings of Saturn know nothing about me," the poet Eryn Green turned to me and said one night as we stood on my porch in the Desert of the Real. "It's the greatest gift I have."

Those sentences form a parable about innovative writing practices. Precisely because dominant modes of narrative know nothing about those (our) practices—their histories, ways of being in the world, interests, ambitions—those practices practice.

Innovative writing can't change cultures, but they can you, me, one skin brush against paper at a time.

the art of unlearning

An undergrad, I used to wander the fiction section of my university library, picking novels off a shelf at random, reading a few lines, skipping, reading.

One evening—I still recall this with a rush of bodily immediacy—I opened Raymond Federman's *Double or Nothing* and abruptly encountered language *mattering* on the page. Encountered words becoming images even as a melancholy comic awareness drifted up within them concerning their own existential problematics. A duet of stories coalesced around almost nothing: a narrator failing to narrate a Jewish immigrant's arrival in the States from postwar Europe.

That's the moment Federman began helping me unlearn writing by making me aware, not simply of *what* it was, but of *how*.

From then on each page for me became canvas and stage.

The traumatic (and ecstatic) rupture of conventional layout in *DoN*'s (no two pages the same, each composed on a typewriter decades before such programs as InDesign appeared) is emblematic of the traumatic (and emancipatory) rupture within *DoN*'s protagonist's (not to mention Federman's) life: the exile from hardwired origins and language.

DoN represents a literary possibility space, an intersemiotic invitation to think about what N. Katherine Hayles calls Media Specific Analysis: the thought that each meta-genre (film, music, etc.) can accomplish things other meta-genres can't, and can't things others can.

By its very presence, Federman's novel-like-object asks:
What is a ~~book~~?
A ~~narrative~~?
How can one ~~write~~ the ~~contemporary~~ rather than ~~rewrite~~ the ~~past~~?

black on black

I remember standing beside him twenty-five years later in the Albright-Knox Art Gallery in Buffalo, New York. We were enjoying his favorite painting: a Clyfford Still, mostly black on black with a small biomorphic red smear in the lower right-hand corner. Federman delighted in it, I imagine, because it was all about itself even as it was all about what every Federman novel is always all about: that small crimson voice in that dark still closet.

I remember us shooting through a Pittsburgh night in 1999 in his Audi packed with participants from the Postmodern Piracy Conference. We were utterly lost, and Federman was utterly unconcerned, and we were it turned out aiming in the wrong direction, and Federman was rambling on, and I, riding shotgun, watched the speedometer crest 80, 85, thinking: *this* is what reading *Double or Nothing* the first time felt like.

For the last dozen years of his life he used to remind me he wanted his epitaph to read (beautifully, preposterously contrary-to-fact): OUT OF PRINT.

Hubert Selby Jnr. — The Room [1971]

GEORGINA HOLLAND

To step into Hubert Selby Jnr.'s *The Room*, is to look into the darkest perversions of the human psyche.

In a visual culture, Selby's prose offers an unsettling return to the written word. Passages are written in such graphic detail, and with such powerful language, that they alone famously made one literary critic physically sick.

For our narrator, a prisoner in solitary confinement, life has the power to 'squeeze your guts out' and to 'suck the blood out of you'.

Selby's prose has the same debilitating power.

Sentences are snapped in half, punctuation and spelling discarded. Paragraphs are left un-ended, the internal monologue is disjointed and delusional. It is a narrative where voices, tones and tenses shout to be heard over one another. We are tossed between the present and past, the real and the imaginary. For our narrator, isolation acts a powerful hallucinogenic. Memories are polluted with the depraved daydreams of an anonymous narrator, who gorges on sadistic fantasies of violent revenge.

Selby reaches deep into the subconscious, extracting the id. What is conventionally taboo and unspoken is cultured and allowed to ferment.

In this book he asks: if left to our own devices, with no sense of guilt or social constraint, would could we produce?

What unspeakable acts lie dormant in the mind of every reader?

Selby's prisoner goes where we dare not. It is in the confines of Selby's solitary cell, just six steps wall-to-wall, that the mind is finally set free.

Who is this 'he'? He is a megaphone for our own perversions.

This is not a film to be turned off; there are no special features, prosthetics, or visual tricks which serve to distance the viewer from what they see—there is no director's cut.

Instead, the graphic rape, murder, and torture scenes are the visual construct of the reader alone, conjured from the shadowy recesses of our own imagination.

We develop the visual narrative, becoming accomplices in the act.

The book horrifies, but it also compels. It is this appeal which speaks volumes about us, the reader.

I defy any reader to tear their eyes from the page, to decide that enough is enough, that Selby has gone too far.

Instead the pages keep turning; we venture, wincing and retching, further into the rabbit hole.

This is a story to be read with a hand over the face, but with eyes peeking from between fingers.

It is a devolution into sadomasochism; each turn of the page is an act of self-flagellation.

Open the door to Selby's room, and unlock your own dissolute phantasms.

What he offers is your own worst nightmares, and they are impossible to refuse.

Now, I dare you not to read it.

Stanley Crawford — *Log of the S.S. the Mrs Unguentine* [1972]

STEPHEN SPARKS

*U*nguentine. The name rolls like a vast Pacific swell, languidly gathering momentum until that sharp last syllable breaks the wave. It's a middle-of-the-sea name; swells like this aren't found near shore. Unimpeded, the wave rises to a towering height, obscuring sun or stars or an indifferent sky, reducing the world to just this: a boat, a woman and her husband, and only a rumor of elsewhere.

Log of the S.S. the Mrs Unguentine, written as an "imaginative blueprint" for a seachange the writer was to undergo in settling down from a life of wandering to a remote farm in New Mexico, is Stanley Crawford's best book. It was written under the influence of the late-60s counterculture but unlike much of the art produced in those years, *Unguentine* has aged well, possibly because our civilization is aging so poorly.

The novel's plot is as simple as a myth: it is an account of the seafaring adventures—which double as the domestic adventures—of Mrs Unguentine, always Mrs, and her husband, a man who "grew nauseous upon land" and so took his wife to sea, fitting out a barge with increasingly elaborate gardens and mechanical contrivances. Over time, the pair become famous (and infamous) in port cities across the world, their home in turn a curiosity, a resort of ill-repute plowing waters out of reach of all legal jurisdiction, a smuggler's ship. The notoriety eventually dissipates, leaving their self-contained barge a floating world unto itself, where the couple, increasingly distant and opaque to each other, carry on as many long-married couples often do, out of inertia, that lingering habit of love.

Crawford specializes in creating petty tyrants, and Unguentine is in many ways the model for those who follow in his later fiction. Unguentine is peripheral but ever-present, a ghost with a bottle in hand haunting these pages while his long-suffering Mrs, uneasy and restless, fills all her days but one, a once-yearly vacation, with chores. Her eponymous prison is an extension or embodiment of herself, a bitter reminder of the isolation of the individual, even or perhaps especially the individual who finds herself in an unequal marriage. The Mrs desires solidity or at least a view of something other than the infinite unbroken horizons of the sea. She finds solace in Unguentine's famed gardens, planted by her husband as much out of a desire for self-reliance as an act of appeasement, though the latter interpretation is undermined by Unguentine's constant tinkering, craftwork that recapitulates the history of man as told in another deceptively simple myth: the Fall. Harmonious nature gives way to technological imitation and life, as we can attest, suffers for it. "I knew I would suffocate with any more lifelessness about," laments the Mrs just before her husband disappears, whether for good or like Odysseus for a ten-year jaunt. With her husband gone, the vessel drifts listlessly until it grows beyond itself, finally finding—that is, creating—the land its mistress so long desired.

Grounded, The Mrs Unguentine loses its purpose. We're stranded there, too, echoing a question posed by the Mrs: "What would it be like to live without the presence of the sea?"

Tom Mallin — Erowina [1972]

NATE DORR

Composed in an apparent fever of first-novel over-ambition, Tom Mallin imbued his debut, *Erowina*, with equal (and overwhelming) parts empathy and formal flair. Erowina is an extremely well-realized character, approached through twenty formally distinct and at times disparate (even contradictory!) portraits, mapping the complete span of a life across body and relationship. If the promise of postmodernism is actually a more complete replication of reality (DFW), such a multifaceted construction implies not formalist remove but warm humanism.

It is with this in mind that I approach the question of authorship in *Erowina*.

Much of the text is presented as Erowina's own: "I stole all of her diaries," Tammy Lamlin tells Gloria Sansum. They are both significant ex-lovers of the bisexual Erowina. "They are not all diaries. Erowina wrote essays, short stories—plays even. They're all there."

And so: Erowina's words, in both fact and fiction, equally true. This self-explanation of the text occurs in the third chapter, "Black Swan Wake", a marathon pub-bound mourning. The preceding coroner's report and funeral could not have been written by Erowina herself. Whereas that first section is entirely impersonal and clinical, in the next sections our heroine gains a retrospective summary identity as "Erowina" in Tammy's the first-person narration. And so we come to know her first as he does. Whether we ever know her otherwise may be somewhat ambiguous.

As Tammy tells us, Erowina's chapters that follow take a variety of formats: first-person stream-of-conscious confessional, symbolic-surreal stories, distanced third-person encounters, two theological dialogues, and, at several points, complicated *mis-en-abyme* cross-cuttings of the entire chronology. One period is conspicuously absent: Tammy's own relationship with Erowina.

"I lie," Tammy admits. "The years fifty-two to fifty-six are missing."

"Convenient," says Gloria.

"I watched her burn them," Tammy offers.

Can this be trusted? It's tempting—Tammy is another sympathetic narrator, and closest to our reader's position outside of Erowina's own life, especially if he has become *de facto* executor of her manuscripts and legacy. But it's awfully convenient that he alone escapes her scrutiny. Mostly at least—we do observe a third-person Erowina ending her relationship, and burning her diaries, in a key life-spanning chapter. But we also learn that Tammy, formerly a doctor, has quit in order to write. Since he has written at least two chapters here, can we ever be sure that he hasn't written them all? He is even seen (in the aforementioned chapter) burning his own autobiographical novel at her request (destroying his side of collective memory). But if this section is in her words then why, after fainting, is she "drawn into awareness by (my) concern and tenderness", a sole intrusion of Tammy's first person into her ostensible narrative sections. The placement is highly deliberate, the questions it raises are integral. Can we even be sure that he burned his own manuscript? That we're not reading it?

I have said before that certainly none of these chapters occurring chronologically after Erowina's death could have been composed in her own words. But is there really any way to know that the scope of her fiction-spinning couldn't extend beyond the horizon of her own life? If Erowina could be Tammy's construction, he could, just as easily, be hers.

Ann Quin — Tripticks [1972]

FRANCIS BOOTH

Ann Quin's *Tripticks*[1], her last completed novel[2] began life as a short story she entered for Ambit Magazine's 1968 competition 'Drugs and the Creative Writer'. It won and was printed in full.[3] In an accompanying letter Quin said:

> This is written under my usual combination of nicotine, caffeine and of course, the birth pill I take—Orthonovin 2.
>
> I should like to emphasise however that although I have never written under the influence of Pot, Peyote, Acid, Hash etc., I am absolutely certain that having taken these, especially Peyote and LSD, they did actually open out a much wider possibility for my writing afterwards

It is her least personal, least internalised, least self-searching novel. Following her visit to Mexico and America, *Tripticks* uses a rhythmic, driving, pop style, 'to write about America, about it being a dream'[4] using cut-ups and fold-ins along the lines of Burroughs and Alan Burns, though the narrative tone of *Tripticks* is perhaps closer to the earlier Burroughs of *Junky* and *Queer*. Quin thought 'in terms of cartoons, each frame changing'[5]; and the novel is illustrated by cartoons[6] like Jeff Nut-

---
1 London: Calder & Boyars, 1972
2 *The Unmapped Country*, about a psychiatric patient: Giles Gordon, ed. *Beyond the Words*. London: Hutchinson, 1975
3 Ambit 35, 1968
4 John Hall, 'Landscape With Three-Cornered Dances': *Guardian* Apr. 29 1972
5 *Tripticks* p. 44
6 The illustrator Carol Annand contributed images of God as a tycoon in glasses to the *Oxford Illustrated Old Testament*, 1968.

tall's novelettes, but based on hard boiled comic strip heroes like Rip Kirby, Steve Roper and Secret Agent X-9, written at one point by Dashiell Hammett.

The narrator speaks like a character from Hammett, James M. Cain, or *Black Mask* magazine—whose covers the illustrations resemble—but in a psychedelic environment and with more existential self-awareness, like a rootless drifter from Bukowski or Fante. This is an 'American' novel in a way that few British experimental novels ever were—Ballard's *The Atrocity Exhibition* and Alan Burns' *Dreamerika!*[7] are rare exceptions.

> In my sophomore year I was considered a clean-cut boy, born of a sturdy woman whose mother once killed 45 Indians with a broom handle. Weaned on moonshine liquor when I was three years old.

Despite the references to comics of the 30s and 40s, *Tripticks*, like Nuttall's *Snipe's Spinster*, is situated where the swinging 60s are becoming the druggy 70s; drugs are everywhere, supplied by the mysterious Nightripper[8].

> I had the feeling that other than the potions Nightripper had handed out he had also passed around something else. The scene resembled a Bosch vision of hell.[9]

Towards the end the writing becomes more internalised, pointing us back to Quin's earlier work and forward to her unfinished novel as the narrator becomes

> a modern day existential hero who is haunted by a world he can neither leave nor take.[10]

---

7 *Tripticks* is dedicated to Alan and Carol Burns.
8 Dr John the Night Tripper released *Gris-Gris* in 1968.
9 p.62.
10 p.189.

Guy Davenport — Taitlin! [1974]

ERIC BYRD

His poetry emerges out of dreams—of a very special kind that abide wholly within the realm of art. (Blok, on Mandelstam)

Guy Davenport's essays are more read than his stories—and such would be the start of a lament, if Davenport's use of the modes were more distinct; if his stories did not abide "wholly within the realm of art"; if his essays and reviews were less visionary, if they were mere journalism, Sunday summaries. But for Davenport criticism carries the demands of storytelling, and vice-versa. Kafka, for instance, is as likely to figure in a story as to form the subject of an essay. In his *Paris Review* interview Davenport revealed that the 'The Hunter Gracchus', an essay on Kafka's story, started out as a story, and 'The Aeroplanes at Brescia', his picture of Kafka's visit to an early exhibition of flying machines, and one of the wonders of *Tatlin!* (1974), started out as an essay. Of his compositions he concluded, "It's all one big happy family."

Davenport's critical prose is sibling to that of his onetime friend and fellow Pound disciple Hugh Kenner, whose *The Pound Era* Davenport hailed as a "new kind of book in which biography, history and analysis of literature are so harmoniously articulated that every page has a narrative sense." Like *The Pound Era*, Davenport's *The Geography of the Imagination: Forty Essays* vividly narrates influential encounters and pungently pictures shocks of recognition. Degas, tracer of haunches equine and balletic, is awake all night with Muybridge's *Zoopraxia*, with its leaping nudes and galloping tarpans. Shelley and his guest, a literary banker, inspect a copy of Diodorus; both are struck by the boastful inscription attributed to a pharaoh whose name a Greek source had garbled to "Ozymandias," and they sit down to their respective sonnets.

In Davenport's stories such scenes are magically magnified, made even stranger. Coming to *Tatlin!* from the essays one finds a personal and particular use of the information. This is Davenport's dreamt world, with its archaic echoes, classical pederasty, and precisely described machines ("the *logos* hides in technology in our time"). Davenport takes a few recoverable facts, second- and third-hand "doubtful certainties," and makes an environment of them, concrete, habitable, and above all, *seen*. He says of 'The Aeroplanes at Brescia':

> *Kafka's account of this event is his first published writing, and as he could not in 1909 know the significance of what he has seen, I combined his newspaper article with Brod's memory of the occasion in his biography of Kafka, and with what I could discover of other people (D'Annunzio, Puccini) who were there, as well as of people who might well have been there (Wittgenstein). To realize certain details I studied the contemporary photographs of Count Primoli, read histories of aviation, built a model of Blériot's Antoinette CV25, and collected as rich a gathering of allusions to the times as I could. I presided over the story like a playful Calvinist God who knew what would happen in years to come.*

Lawrence Durrell — The Avignon Quintet [1974-1985]

NADINE MAINARD

If, in an assemblage of ruminations on the works of lesser-known authors who collectively are characterised by their willingness to play with the form of the novel as the means to manufacture content, who refuse the simplistic Event A acting on Person B producing Consequence C influencing Outcome D and so on until Conclusion Z, otherwise known as the plot or action-driven linear novel, who experiment with the intersection and amalgamation of insights from other disciplines and incorporate these in the creation of *story*, and who happily blur the line between phiction and phact, filosofy and herstory, logic and linguistic, psyens and *Ars*, and onto logy: epistemology and teleology, Lawrence Durrell's *magnum opus The Avignon Quintet* were to be excluded, the only reasonable tenet for such an omission would be his relative notoriety as the correspondent of Henry Miller, for his self-publication of his first novel, for his brother Gerald's tongue-in-cheek depiction of Lawrence's youth in the latter's memoir, and for the commercial and critical success of his "modernist" and most-lauded work *The Alexandria Quartet (Justine, Balthazar, Mountolive, Clea)*. In short, Lawrence Durrell is *not* unknown, albeit not for exploratory acts of fiction, nor for the fact that "Christine Brooke-Rose could be heard merely dismissing him mildly as 'poor Durrell'."[i]

The Avignon Quintet, a series of five double-titled[ii] novels: *Monsieur or The Prince of Darkness, Livia or Buried Alive, Constance or Solitary Practices,*

---

i Brown, Keith, *Sightings: Selected Literary Essays*, Peter Lang, 2008, pp251-252
ii The structure of the *Quintet*'s chapters follows: five, nine, fifteen plus one, ten, and eight. The double titling of each novel suggests double authoring, while the third name (given to the entire work) hints at another author.

Sebastian or Ruling Passions, Quinx or The Ripper's Tale, however, has remained commercially and critically ignored, and due in substantial part to the canonisation of a Durrell labelled and thence discarded as "modernist"[iii]. The label can be considered ludicrous when applied to *The Avignon Quintet,* and dubious in the context of *The Alexandria Quartet,* given that Durrell prefaced a US edition of *Balthazar* with a reluctant[iv] admission concerning the conceit of the *Quartet:* its structure derived from a rejection of linearity in terms of time and space, and an attempt to transmute a non-specialist's understanding of Einstein's Theory of Relativity (as an artificial construct) to a literary form. The two novels *Justine, Balthazar,* are the same story narrated from the same first-person perspective, however the latter is draped with the observations (corrections) of a character from the former; *Mountolive* is related from the perspective of a minor character from *Justine* and *Balthazar,* overlaying the political perspective of the period and treating the self-significant first-person narrator of *Justine* and *Balthazar* as a bit-part player in a grander scheme; and the fourth novel, *Clea,* is the offspring of the first three "siblings", completing a circular return to the principal character having evolved as the artist to which an earlier self aspired at the commencement of the *Quartet.* Each perspective is always undermined by the presence of either its own transformation or the intrusion of another. Reality is thus dependent on the I of the beholder.

While criticism of the *Quartet* assumes a preoccupation with the modernist theme of a search for meaning, the attention to form displayed in the *Quartet,* as well its use of various narrative techniques, lack of linearity, and deliberate obfuscation of an authoritative interpretation of perspective, suggest not only postmodernist leanings but critical reluctance to examine these. If Mannerism is contemporary

---

iii Durrell suffers now for the unfortunate sexism colouring *The Alexandria Quartet,* thus rendering him unpalatable to feminist studies. However, among other influences, he was imbued with the doctrine of Freud " . . . Freud and Einstein preside over the fates of [the characters] . . ." in *The Alexandria Quartet,* (Durrell, Conversations, p231), and in part his work can be viewed as an attempt to resolve the conflict created by conditioning (women as objects), the legacy of Freud (refusal to accept the emotional, spiritual, physical, and mental emancipation of women) and the increasing actuality of that emancipation, as well as the influence of *Tao* teachings in his later years.
iv *Ibid,* p257

Postmodernism[v], and Durrell is a Mannerist writer[vi], the lack of a postmodernist appraisal of *The Avignon Quintet* may be attributed to an instance of the same phenomenon which ultimately marginalised Christine Brooke-Rose: a writer's transgression of literary labels and categories makes poor subject matter for academic studies and marketing campaigns.

While no character in *The Alexandria Quartet* ever crosses the footlights to address the audience directly during the omniscient narrator's delivery, the reader must be acutely conscious of the first-person narrative technique used as the device addressing her/him and prodding a consideration of the novel as an artifice, or of the comments made by the *Quartet*'s pre-eminent writer Pursewarden with respect to "truth disguised as fiction"; *roman-a-clef* is an accepted technique for violating ontological barriers[vii].

The Avignon Quintet evinces many of the stylistic hallmarks of a postmodern text, apart from Durrell's delight in languages; he is "... at play in a field of words, ideas, and forms ... [violating] the basic rules of the verbal game ..."[viii]. The propensity for integrating mathematical concepts (or indeed scientific theorising) is deployed to meticulous and evident effect (characteristic of the OuLiPo): amorous relationships are typically triangular or multiples of triangles, while the connections between the characters suggest a pentagon (an n-gon where n = 5): Piers, Sylvie and Bruce are the triangle, Sabine and Toby complete the pentagon, or Pia and Sutcliffe, or Blanford and the Duchess, in *Monsieur*, and variations on these characters in subsequent books follow the numerical groupings (as the work unfolds, the genesis of the characters blurs further through shuffled pronouns and flits between free indirect discourse and quoted passages—who is the creator, who is the created,

---

v   Fullbrook, Kate, 'Whose Postmodernism?', in Dowson, Jane & Earnshaw, Steven (eds) *Postmodern Subjects, Postmodern Texts*, Rodopi, 1995, p81
vi   Steiner, George, 'Lawrence Durrell: The Baroque Novel', in Moore, Harry T (ed) *The World of Lawrence Durrell*, Southern Illinois University Press, 1962, pp13-23
vii   Mchale, Brian, *Constructing Postmodernism*, Routledge, 2012, p153
viii   Godshalk, William L., 'Lawrence Durrell's Game in *The Avignon Quartet*' in Begnal, Michael H (ed), *On Miracle Ground: Essays on the Fiction of Lawrence Durrell*, Associated University Press, 1990, p187.

reflecting the wave-particle duality of quantum mechanics[ix]); the work is the only exemplar in the English speaking world[x] to attempt to create an interrelated and connected sequence of five novels modelled on the geometry of a *quincunx*[xi]; the narratives of the books are highly fragmented and evolve similarly to the blossoming of a-periodic fractals (regular pentagon tilings cannot tessellate); the first book has a material beginning (words on a page numbered one) but those same beginning words i.e. *beginning of the story* are repeated on a later page to demonstrate the beginning of the story is some time, some place other, while the final page of the *Quintet* presents the quintessential bifurcation of chance to refute any definitive conclusion i.e. an horizon of potential, and this palimpsestic method of looping and reworking saturates all five novels, even while still conveying a story; the authority of the text is undermined by its reliance on the pre-texts to which it alludes or which are contained therein (and suggesting an *ur*-text), thereby reminding the reader of the act of writing as well as the artifice; and finally, Durrell's attribution to Wordsworth opening the last volume *Quinx* that artistic endeavour ". . . must itself create the taste by which it is to be judged . . ." both acknowledges the exploratory nature of the entire work while signifying no less to the reader: in other words, all that has preceded has been necessary to cultivate in the reader the sensibility to and appreciation for what has been (and will be) achieved in the *The Avignon Quintet*.

Remembering the recursive nature of *Between*, *Remake* and *Life, End of*, or the spatial depiction of London and loners via the alphabet and transitions between the interior voices of the homeless characters in *Next*, or the overt indebtedness (worship) of characters to the Reader as God (Durrell puns dog but leaves Anubis for another day) borrowed and

---

[ix] Discussed at length by Lorenz, in 'Quantum Mechanics and the Shape of Fiction: "Non-Locality" in the Avignon Quincunx', Lorentz, Paul H., *Weber Studies*, Vol. 14, No. 1, 1997.

[x] A handful of stand-alone novels have also used the symbolism of the quincunx on which to model narrative structures (eg Charles Palliser's *The Quincunx*) but none are an integrated set of novels, each of which is its own quincunx, as is *The Avignon Quintet*.

[xi] A quincunx is a geometric arrangement of five points formed as a cross, four positioned as a square or rectangle, and the fifth placed at the centre of the point. In three dimensions, the central point would be the apex of a pyramid.

recycled from more books than could be imbibed in an ordinary reading lifetime in *Textermination*, and the mischievous witticisms of *Amalgamemnon* and *Verbivore*, Christine Brooke-Rose may have been nothing more than backhanding herself if she truly spurned Durrell as undeserving of esteem as a writer of innovative and thought-provoking fiction.

Christine Brooke-Rose — Thru [1975]

DAVID DETRICH

THE PERSONIFICATION OF NARRATIVE SELF FLIRTING WITH THE FIGURE IN RED GARTERS

"The glossy surface of black ink contrasts the mirrored pages in semantic echoes : : the sentence structures convey the voice of the narrator who envisions the image of a woman on her knees gathering a white liquid in a small cup / the essence of love is splashed across the smile of the morning sky while Venus ascends above the nearby stars," the novelist sits at his desk with the gradual hypnotrance of hot cocoa moods blown by the winter winds across the glazed dark green coffee cup, reminiscent of a Christine Brooke-Rose green, as the glossy surface of black ink transforms into a minimalist avant-garde text with white mini-marshmallow rock formations metamorphosing into blue tinted snowdrifts / flirting with the lady in red garters who ascends towards the Willem de Kooning painting / the exertion of love is heard in the panting of breath / one man gathers what another man spills . . .

"The electronic circuitry of the abstract painterly form tunes in to the Phil Lesh bass lines which express the subtle painted rhythmic textures in broad brush strokes inspiring the falcon headed novelist who admires the double breasted curves of the supermodel bursting with love / bubbles ascend with the golden shudder of earrings blowing a kiss towards the Surrealist pipedream who is the square-shouldered light of the candle flame / a window reflection enlarged into snow crystals falling on the raspberry chocolate mousse / which morphs into the golden square of the photogenic identity in a relationship with the flirtatious pink flower petal figurative drawing," the sweetness of caramelespresso * sleekthighs * wingsfluttering above the pillowpatterns of the eroticphantasy * nymphomania * bottoms up, babe to the crack of light from the cool shades of the nightlife, as you blow out the candle flame while making a date with the abstract curves of the orange ladybug with black dots which shudder in the winter nightfall with the cute gesture of an audible kiss to the erect form of the narrator / that's me magnifying the light of the lens . . .

"I admire the soothing syllogism of your sensual motion which arouses the symbolic abstract form as the personification of narrative self to express admiration for the sex star whose sleek thighs in stockings inspire the red Valentine heart of the phenomenal novelist / to recite poetry to the cool wind in the Superior breeze the abstract personification of vanity breathes smoke rings as the airplane ascends above the city with a Robert Delaunay puff into clouds / Cecil Taylor blowing the whistle the better to appreciate the brilliant mind of chaotic bubbles bursting with electronic circuitry / to defuse the situation while whale watching with wizardry whirling wishes the panting breath which transforms into a book of vaporous mist read before the windows withdrawn into self / your golden bangles stratagem blows my mind with the figurative drawing of a dinosaur lady wearing a fluffy white Santa Claus tiara below the green apple tree which branches into rounded green abstract leaf symmetries of infinity / the ancient map cartography of the western states appears visible as a cow's head under the upward curving bow symbol while the conceptual form of Laurentia exists as a precise foreshadowing of the Great Lakes," a fictive relationship with Nombres begins as love shudders in the curves of goldensquare * textcolumns * Surrealist pipedreams metamorphosing into a photogenic pillowcase which could be drawn as a snowdrift becoming a waft of apple fritters which evolve into a floating island of chocolate raspberry mousse rhythmic ambiance . . .

Georges Perec — An Attempt at Exhausting a Place in Paris [1975]

LAUREN ELKIN

Date: 14/11/14
Time: 12:01 pm
Place: Café de la Mairie, Place Saint-Sulpice, Paris
Weather: intermittent rain, grey skies, slightly cold

I convened my students here today to ask them to "play Perec" by attempting to exhaust this place in Paris. It's around the same time of year that he came, but forty years later; he was here on 18, 19, and 20 October in 1974, and today is the 14th of November 2014. If you factor in global warming, our November's probably much the same as his October. I try to imagine Perec sitting where I'm sitting, with his wild hair and his wild beard, scribbling his notes on graph paper, developing "an obsessive fear of apple green 2CVs." Would he approve of my bringing thirty American undergraduates to imitate him, typing their notes into their iPhones? Would he approve of me, sitting in the café, watching over them?

I've never been one for imitating literary devices. Just as Perec's anti-hero Gaspard realizes in *Le Condottiere*, it's impossible to recreate someone else's masterpiece, merely by imitating their technique. So much of art is a product of your own time and place. I guess that's what this exercise is about. Collapsing the distinction between art and life.

But in this case the device dovetails with what I'd probably be doing anyway, left to my own devices. I don't think I'll ever get tired of writing down what I see around me in Paris; it will always be fascinating to sit in a café and watch people. It answers some deep human need to look at other people and what they're doing. Unabashed nosiness. For sure it's the impulse behind reality television, the direct line from Woolf's old lady in the corner opposite to Perec to *Made in Chelsea*. The woman sitting next to me is eating meat and potatoes for lunch, washing it down with a pint of beer, yet she looks like someone's bougie grandma. A man with an earnest expression on his face enters, dressed all in black, wheeling a suitcase behind him. Someone in the back room has ordered a glass of Brouilly, the waiter tells the barman. An older woman in expensive sneakers stands at the bar drinking an espresso with another older woman who is also wearing expensive sneakers.

If I see an apple-green 2CV I'll be very surprised.

How did Perec do it? The sheer amount of data all around us at every moment is staggering. How to give it form? And he didn't have himself to use as a model. I try to be more schematic. It's raining outside. Every two people have umbrellas, every third person doesn't. Those people sometimes have hoods, sometimes don't. One person carries his umbrella. Is it broken? Many people, umbrella'd or not, dart past the cafe, or hurry in and stand in the entrance, for a moment, adjusting.

The square is dotted with my students. I wonder how they're finding the activity. I wonder if they're bored. They connected with Perec in the warmth of the classroom. Out in the world, I wonder how it translates.

In class when we talked about this text we focused on the epistemological questions it raises. How can we know, I began to ask. *Anything*, one student filled in. How can we know anything, yes, I said, even the things happening around us. We look at the birds and we don't see the people. We look at the buses and we don't see the birds. Where to look? What's important? Is "important" even the right word? How to make sense of it? Look at the way he lists those buses, another student said. No way they happened to form those patterns. He obviously took his notes and revised them, said the student next to her. They look like poetry. Look at this book of poetry he's written.

Fernando del Paso — Palinuro of Mexico [1976]

IGNACIO M. SÁNCHEZ PRADO

Published originally in 1976, *Palinuro of Mexico* is one of the towering achievements of Latin American fiction. Even though Dalkey Archive Press has an English-language version in circulation, and despite the author's fame in literary circles in Spanish, it still remains one of the most underappreciated masterpieces of modern literature. The reasons are clear: it does not correspond to the type of magical-realist or gritty fiction usually expected by readers of Latin American fiction (too informed in their taste by Borges, García Márquez, and Bolaño), while many Mexican readers are more familiar with his other masterwork, *News from the Empire*, a historical novel concerned with Maximilian and Charlotte of Habsburg's rule of Mexico, and the most important work of the genre in recent Latin American history.

However, *Palinuro of Mexico* is one of those must-read books that struggle to find a general readership due to its aesthetic boldness and its literary experimentation. The book focuses on a medicine student who is killed during the Tlatelolco massacre of October 2, 1968. But this description in fact obscures the book. Rather than providing a realist or a political novel, the book is a sprawling literary representation of the spirit of Mexico's youth in the 1960s, informed by the sexual revolution, the appropriation of cosmopolitan culture, and political mobilization. The result is an experimental novel that draws heavily from British satirical traditions (Jonathan Swift and Laurence Sterne are explicitly referenced), Italian *Commedia dell'arte* (the chapter where Palinuro is killed is a 100-page long play in this style) and Rabelaisian excess. The character himself is named after a pilot in the *Aeneid*, whose bones are never buried. But the point of the novel is not solely to mourn the loss of young people in the Tlatelolco massacre, but also to remember them through the joyful, lusty, and beautiful life that they pursued.

The book contains many wonders, which readers are invited to unpack. Chapters include a beautiful sexual exploration between Palinuro and his beloved Estefanía, the mourning of a dead mirror, a Gulliverian journey through islands that also are advertising agencies, a narration of Palinuro's grandparents in World War I, amongst other fascinating and at times indescribable occurrences. It is a novel filled with a joy that literature rarely imparts: the bliss of a life discovering all the little and big dimensions of the world expressed through the pleasure of a literary form full of surprises and intensities. Instead of providing what the canon of Mexican literature has typically given us (Mexicanness, disappointment with the Revolution, disengaged cosmopolitanism), *Palinuro of Mexico* captures its period in full, in its enjoyments and its pains.

Coleman Dowell — Island People [1976]

EUGENE H. HAYWORTH

When Coleman Dowell's riveting novel Island People was published in 1976, critics compared it to T.S. Eliot's The Waste Land, based in part on its complex, shifting points of view. Many contemporaries, including John Kuehl and Gilbert Sorrentino (who both taught the novel in postmodern literature classes), Ihab Hassan, and Walter Abish, praised the book. Edmund White's review in the New York Times called it "a work of art" and said that Dowell had "evidenced courage and invention in creating a work of art so original and difficult as to be alive to baffling and baffled perceptions."[1]

An entry in Dowell's journal dated April 8, [1974] provides a rich portrait of the writer at work. "I'm at a standstill on ISLAND PEOPLE. It now numbers over three hundred pages and the individual sections are very good, but there is the problem of putting the mosaic pieces together into a workable whole. I know what I want but haven't quite yet found the method, as two possibilities are there: a fuller scheme; a more fragmented scheme. Either would work and I wait for the desire that SHOULD come, to come and settle the matter for me . . ."

Dowell's publisher, New Directions, described the work as "an allegorical fiction—largely in the form of private journal entries and short stories exchanged in a literary duel—that chronicles a bitter, defeated man's journey toward emotional tranquility."[2] Many reviewers remarked on the fragmentary nature of the novel. Dowell was concerned with the psychological insight he could bring to his characters, and Island People explores the anxiety and paranoia that might result when an

---

[1] White, Edmund. (1976, September 19) Review of Island People by Coleman Dowell. New York Times Book Review, p. 40.
[2] News From New Directions. [Circa 1976].

individual lives in isolation. *Island People* is a complex, horrifying tale filled with puzzles, enigmas, and ambiguities. The narrator, a middle-aged, gay playwright, moves to a farmhouse on an island where he spends time writing stories and keeping a diary. He has left New York to seek refuge from the violence of the city. Like Dowell's earlier novel *Mrs. October*, the work itself comments on the novel form as characters become narrators who invent other characters. These narrators are unreliable and hard to identify. One might approach the novel as a series of stories presented by one unnamed narrator, or view it as a dialogue between two aspects of the narrator's psyche.

Like other works of postmodern fiction, Dowell provides clues that suggest a strategy for reading the novel. First, he carefully describes the difference between the narrator's style and that of the narrator's alter ego Beatrix, and gives a further clue in the fact that each writer uses a different name for the pet dachshund: Beatrix refers to the dog as "Miss Gold" or the "bitch" while the narrator uses the designation "my lady." The narrator refers to himself solely with the first person pronoun; however, Beatrix identifies him as "Chris." In the opening section, IS-LAND PEOPLE, the author describes the book to come, which will take the form of a diurnal narrative written in third person, journal entries in the first person, a "translation of experience" written in all persons, and a nocturnal narrative. There are also typographical clues to denote the book's sections: an ornate Victorian symbol and a change in typeface indicate the ongoing ghost story; sections written in italics, or whose titles are in CAPS, are authored by Beatrix. Finally, the characters occasionally address messages to each other directly.

In 'Some Remarks on *Island People*' Gilbert Sorrentino sees the act of writing presented in the book as both an act of salvation and one of exorcism of "the ghost of self."[3] The artificial nature of fiction is nowhere more clearly conveyed than in the fact that *Island People* is a book within *Island People*. Sorrentino explains this as "Dowell's commentary on the novel as a closed system.[4] And in 'Time Frames: Temporality and Narra-

---

3 Sorrentino, Gilbert. (1982), Some Remarks on *Island People*. *Review of Contemporary Fiction* 2(3): 122.
4 *Ibid* p. 123.

tion in Coleman Dowell's *Island People'*, Ursula K. Heise examines the narrative structure of the novel in relationship to its multiple frames. Heise concludes that the novel "takes the process of narrative framing to its limits, projecting, in a movement of inverted *mise en abyme*, its own frame into itself."[5]

As Dowell described it, he is "one man writing about every aspect of himself and trying to become a peninsula because he's so tired of being an Island."[6] The process of disentangling those multiple selves is key to understanding this complex novel, and Dowell's thick prose deserves much further consideration.

---

5   Heise, Ursula K. (1991), Time Frames: Temporality and Narration in Coleman Dowell's *Island People*. *The Journal of Narrative Technique*, 21, (3): 279.
6   O'Brien, John. (1982). A Conversation with Coleman Dowell By John O'Brien. 2(3): 87.

Raymond Federman — Take It or Leave It [1976]

STEVE KATZ

I first met Ray Federman when I taught at Cornell. We invited him to read. That was the time of DOUBLE OR NOTHING and he gave a good reading. As we were about to enter a restaurant later he asked my companion, obviously an intimate friend, "Wouldn't you rather sleep with a Frenchman?" Federman's accent was as if on a rheostat, which for seduction he dialed to maximum French. Anyone committing to read his long bizarre (a French word) simple complicated novel TAKE IT OR LEAVE IT gets to "sleep with a Frenchman". One of the earliest gestures that the tenacious narrative voice makes is to drop several buckets from his literary frontloader—names of his novelist peers, critics, literary predecessors, theorists (mostly French), all fomenting in his purview. They string out along the line of his voice like charms on a bracelet. He translates a well known passage from Derrida, and presents it as a typographical medallion in the center of a page. He assures us from the start that the author is well-educated, and is equal to any challenge literary or theoretical as Federman presents an Epic that unfolds "Frenchy's" adventures in the 82nd Airborne, and his assimilation into USA.

The voice toggles to an expletive-packed vernacular that flings contempt at his cohorts in the 82nd, and most of the others who cross the crappy path. The acceleration and momentum recalls Céline, particularly when he punctuates with Célinesque ellipses. Frenchy intends to see the USA in his battered Buick, while he heads for an assignment at Fort Drum where a paycheck waits. He nimbly bends his expletive packed line through conflicts with the officers commissioned and non-, adventures in Jazz, sexual diversions, alcohol mischief, and other digressions, an admirable picaresque in this vernacular tour de force.

The line he grips winds through typographical adventures, perhaps too often on the level of visual pun, but showing his almost giddy pleasure the author takes casting the line of the book. Whenever the narrator whips into the revelatory or the absurd or the frivolous, Frenchy manages to hang on. The characters he condemns rarely talk for themselves. Not a scene is freed from authorial control. Though he advocates the casual he keeps a tight rein along the protracted seam of iteration. A mystery how it becomes so compelling though repetitious, and full of offensive stereotypes, and so obvious in his self-aggrandizing exaggeration and fabrication? Some centripetal force keeps us clinging.

What keeps you reading is perhaps the feeling that you witness the flailing of a man drowning in his own suds, trying to stay alive in the hidden undertow. Maybe it's schadenfreude. It's like watching Buster Keaton. The narrator grips the line to save himself. You hang on too as if a literary breakthrough is about to unspool. When he threads into WWII, his life threatened through the Vichy Government and the holocaust, an unanticipated gravitas drenches the novel, even in retrospect. You nudge closer to the narrator, on a new level of sympathy and understanding. The desperate pace has power and credibility as the narcissism becomes an assertion by Frenchy that he is still alive despite it all, and will be as long as he continues to spin the line, grasp it, and pull himself along his story as he makes it. This darkening of the voice makes TAKE IT OR LEAVE IT one of the most moving, original books of the late XXth century. It deepens the tone of postmodern self-reflexivity, and takes it beyond antics.

Federman continued to explore that material, WWII and survival during the holocaust. THE VOICE IN THE CLOSET, for instance. The material became money for him, particularly in Europe. When I occasionally saw him at conference or reading he loved to tell me how much money he got for an appearance in Antwerp, for instance.

"They paid me in cash," said he.

My last dance with Federman was at a reading I was to give at Chapman University in Orange, CA. He had retired into golf in San Diego at the time. Mark Axelrod asked Raymond to introduce me. A substantial crowd showed up. Federman's introduction took most of an hour, during which he hardly mentioned me, but spoke about Federman. By the time I staggered to the podium, and stood in the vortex of "himself", most of the audience was gone. I read anyway to a chosen few. Take it or leave it.

Italo Calvino — *If on a winter's night a traveller* [1979]

SILVIA BARLAAM

I am sitting here now to write a short piece about Italo Calvino and his *If on a winter's night a traveller* and I wonder at the genius of this man, who wrote a book about readers and writers and publishers and authors and all the possibilities in between, a book where many stories begin and never end, where each story is a different story, a crime a thriller a romance a diary a detective adventure, genre morphing into style morphing into technique morphing into content, and where each story has the same reader yet a different reader, where the love for a woman drives the whole as it has been since the beginning of time (allegedly) and every woman is the same woman and every writer is seeking for truth and story and love and at the end, at the end there is a book, and a reader, and a writer.

Every potential position of a given reader in respect to any given story is examined: the careful reader, the distracted one; the reader that needs to read it all preferably in one go and the reader that just browses; the reader that looks for a specific type of story always and the one that keeps changing her mind about the story being sought; the reader who hunts for deeper and hidden meaning whether it's there or not and the reader who takes words at face value.

What would you do in reading this? Would this piece of writing meet your expectations of a Calvino review? Would you expect to see more factual information, more data, his life history, his motivations and passions? Or would you rather have a glimpse of all that he's written, a quick recap of his books and life work, a list of titles and dates? What type of reader are you?

And what type of writer am I? Am I summarizing a literary theory, an ideology of words and books, in 500 words? Am I seeking to portray a faithful vision of this particular book and author and the ideas supporting his structure? Am I that good a writer, or that bad?

There's a book, written by Italo Calvino, titled *If on a winter's night a traveller*. It takes you on a great journey and you will want to read it more than once and find another reader with whom to discuss it and on the way you'll learn a lot about the power and magic of the written word and how, in such expert hands, it can rewrite itself over and over and always be new, and wonderful, and profound.

Gilbert Sorrentino — Mulligan Stew [1979]

M.J. NICHOLLS

Imagining myself looking at myself, I seem to be relaxed.*
(p.9)

Gilbert Sorrentino's *Mulligan Stew* is one of the Great Comic Novels and a hack-seeking exocet missile in the War Against Cliché. The novel recasts Antony Lamont from Flann O'Brien's *At Swim-Two-Birds* as an arrogant, self-described avant-garde novelist, chronicling his hilarious descent to writerly oblivion. Lamont considers his first published work, *Three Deuces*—a pompous crime potboiler—to be among the Great Works of American literature. His follow-up novel *Guinea Red* (later *Crocodile Tears*) is labelled a Sur-Neofictional mystery and ups the ante in the indulgent, ponderous hackwork stakes. Sorrentino worked as an editor for Grove Press in the 1960s (helping elevate Hubert Selby to stardom), and exacts his revenge with these exquisite and riotous parodies of arrogant, overwritten, inelegant prose styles that make embarrassing gropes for the profound. Fourteen chapters of Lamont's MS appear in *MS* and leave the reader rib-tickled and breathless in equal quantities—delirious exhaustion is this novel's MO.

I did my best to leer appreciatively, while my heart twisted in me like a boiling lobster. (p50)

Sorrentino modelled his structure on *At Swim-Two-Birds*, and expands upon O'Brien's metafictional innovations with his characters plotting to escape from Lamont's novel as the author loses control of his mind and

---

* Gilbert Sorrentino, *Mulligan Stew*, Dalkey Archive Press, 1996.

MS. The weaving of intertextual references (characters are taken from O'Brien, James Joyce, and Dashiell Hammett), and the fondness for the relentless and freewheeling list (and there are a maddening number of lists) are homages to and continuations of Joyce's vast literary legacy, as evidenced by his appearance in 'The Masque of Fungo' (a 40-page play indebted to the Circe chapter of *Ulysses*).

> Ugo colored, blanched, then colored again and blenched. (p53)

Among the copious delights are letters Lamont writes to his sister Sheila, ranting about the novel and his loathing for the successful and talented Dermot Trellis. There are bizarre parodies of academic mathematical papers, sophomoric erotic poems ('The Sweat of Love'), and spam letters from two Mexican seducers, Corrie and Berthe, with whom Lamont becomes obsessed, and a late descent into middle-English (presaging the archaic forms Sorrentino parodies in his inventive if less successful novel *Blue Pastoral*).

> At that moment her face took on the unmistakeable frown that one gets on a face when one smells gas. (p232)

Mulligan Stew launches its assault on cliché, bad writing, writer egos, and literature as a capitalistic commodity, themes prevalent across Sorrentino's career and in his incisive criticism (see *Something Said*), with an unrelenting blast of the original and unexpected: this masterpiece demonstrates a spellbinding comic imagination in full flight and a tireless passion for formal and artistic innovation—a lesson in what to strive for as a writer, a warning in what to sidestep as a writer, and a rewarding feast for the daring and willing reader. *MS* deserves to be savoured and re-read for generations.

> Just the sounds that filled the dim boudoir were enough to make the thick honey of Amour flow copiously from the pounding beam I sedulously larrupped! (p326)

Roald Dahl — The Twits [1980]

HAROLD LAD

ADDRESS TO THE CLEAN-SHAVEN CLUB ANNUAL DINNER 2015:

I do decree, my shaven brethren, that we are living in a post-*Twits* society, where the bearded man is King: alpha-male, femme-magnet, and prickle-faced surveyor of his universe. During the Cold War, the beard was a symbol of Russian evil and the sort of scowl-laden badness as depicted in Dahl's magnum opus. In the 1960s, middle-class dropouts hopped up on mescaline sat Indian-style before their über-hippie Godfather Allan Ginsberg, and into the 1970s prog rock bands retreated inside their facial hair to hide from their mediocrity. The 1980s found the beard in its least popular phase (Dahl's novel was released in 1980 and helped precipitate this beard armistice), worn only by pop stars such as George Michael and Kenny Loggins desperate to cultivate a rebel chic. This blissful period lasted through the 1990s and the early 2000s, until the beard made a stealth return through the youth culture and beyond. Now, my chin-smooth chums, I am sure the following is familiar. I live on a street where beards represent power, popularity, and magnetic sexual attraction. En route to work each morning, I must endure small talk with some smug character named Gregor. I fight to keep cool as his mouth, encased in a ratty blonde beard, makes vapid words while his beautiful girlfriend stares lovingly into his eyes, and after the torture, the two putter off in their souped-up Subaru as I release a hail of expletives into the beige walls. These are the pains we face, dear brothers. The beard must be obliterated. These new beard-sporting menaces tend to share similar characteristics: avid listeners to Keane or Admiral Fallow, the tendency to consider William Burroughs the pinnacle of exploratory fiction, a preference for tapas bars manned by un-Spanish dicks named Dan, and an inactive membership to the Liberal Democrats. These phonies affect to straddle high and middlebrow culture, feigning an interest in Japanese Noh theatre or Brechtian cabaret, while secretly playing Candy Crush on their iphones or downloading the latest Jake Bugg single. Why are women so attracted to these bearded swine? It takes a certain sort of bland and primped-up middlebrow hipster-bore to fall in love with the bearded. So, my brethren, I am saying today, let this be a call to arms (or beards). Let us implement our plan to cure the bearded in their beds during National Drug-and-Shave Day, and we can return to Dahl's proposed utopia. Tomorrow, you will venture into the world with your scissors and razors, and make history. Some detractors will scoff and call us loonies or crackpots. Spurn their scorn! This is our moment to take up the gleaming instruments of change, apply them to the hairy faces of fate, and create the unstubbled chins of promise. Onward, soldiers!

Donald Barthelme — Sixty Stories [1981]

LEE KLEIN

Worst of all is to begin. All was dark until Donald Barthelme lit me up. A Luciferian aleph illuminated those collections of sixty and forty stories. Books like these need to come at the right time. If read before I encountered the dominant realist trend in college (imagine a world ruled by Carver acolytes), I may not have needed playful, bawdy, joyfully obscure, fractured delights that resist the temptation to follow the rational path of entertainment. Like 1960s Vaudevillian cabaret rendered in text, with old-timey cutouts, a simple line drawing of a hand, the word "butter" presented 87 times in a row, something of a sensibility and wit that may have excelled at the Playboy mansion, everything (language-related affections, particularly) seemed airborne —and sometimes even juggled. Characters named Cardinal Y, Edward Lear, Montezuma, Eugénie Grandet, Robert Kennedy (K.), the Emperor, Shotwell, Celeste populate these pages. "Flights of white meat" that move through the sky of Paraguay ("not the Paraguay that exists on our maps") are a metaphor for clouds, or maybe actual strips of chicken/pork. In some ideal alternate reality, Terry Gilliam of the Monty Python cartoons brought these short stories to the big screen.

Was there really once a world in which *The New Yorker* published such things? A few years out of college, unaware of the existence of these stories, I resisted the "creative writing" world based on intuition and exposure to a class called Creative Writing 101. My teacher (a famously committed Carverite) wanted me to write about drink and divorce, I sensed, but oh how I wish he'd slipped me some Barthelme. When I found these stories I recognized a standard to bear as I followed the lead of my ignorant instinct. Situationally depressed, so often bed-bound with books, I could have been swayed by forces more likely to deprave and corrupt than metafiction. I now understand that I was in training, preparing for what was to come. A few years later when George Saunders and DFW emerged, Leyner too, I was ready, and I knew they knew Barthelme.

Middles are nowhere to be found. Same as the first sentence of this, that's a phrase in the last line of a Barthelme story called 'The Dolt', about a guy prepping for his National Writers' Examination to earn his certificate. If my intro to these stories marked my beginning, Barthelme was nowhere to be found in the middle of my story. I rarely read him for years but still, as the patron saint of contemporary literary unconventionality, I invoked his name whenever I sensed his presence. Unpredictability, inventiveness, striking juxtaposition, spirit, these matter more than rising action, climax, resolution—that was the lesson. At the time I first read these stories someone had taped a handwritten sign to the door of our apartment building that said "All Doors Are Open for Exit on the Seventh Floor." I wrote a story based on it. All my doors opened outward thanks to what I was reading.

Endings are elusive. Another phrase in the last line of 'The Dolt'. Now when I read these stories I fear some of my doors have closed. I zone out after a few pages. Jokes land nary a laugh. Pop references seem distant and obscure. But that's OK. All's as it should be, actually. It's clear these stories are no longer what I need, but without them I never would have become the dolt I am today.

Alexander Theroux — *Darconville's Cat* [1981]

STEVEN MOORE

Though often grouped with maximalist, encyclopedic novels because of its elaborate style and range of references, Theroux's novel differs from others of that species (Gaddis's *Recognitions*, Pynchon's *Gravity's Rainbow*) in being the easiest to read. The story is simple, the plot unfolds in linear fashion, and the moral is clear. It's a rare, perhaps unique, example of a novel that reads like a bestseller while deploying the kind of literary pyrotechnics associated with rarified postmodern fiction.

Boy meets girl, boy loses girl and vows revenge, comes to his senses and erects this literary cathedral to unrequited love, before romantically dying in Venice. Betrayed by the Isabel Rawsthorne, Alaric Darconville devotes himself to the true love of his life, the English language. The language is unusually rich, employs an arsenal of rhetorical devices, and revives words that haven't been used in hundreds of years. As the dust-jacket boasts, "Its chapters embody a multiplicity of narrative forms, including a diary, a formal oration, an abecedarium, a sermon, a litany, a blank-verse play, poems, essays, parodies, and fables." Playing on a popular phrase, the chapter entitled "What Is One Picture Worth?" contains exactly one thousand words. The black page of grief from *Tristram Shandy* is here and enough literary allusions to keep an annotator occupied for years tracking them down. It's by turns funny and sad, satiric and mournful.

It's a performance piece, to be sure, taking full advantage of "the opportunity for display that [novels] offered a good mind," as the Canon in *Don Quixote* says, "providing a broad and spacious field where one's pen could write unhindered. . . ." But Theroux's lavish style and far-flung allusions are functional as well: Darconville is well-read, richly imaginative, and individualistic, whereas the girl he falls for . . . isn't. A simple soul who wants to play it safe and consequently dumps Darconville for a local boy, Isabel's plain language and lack of imagination is stylistically at odds with the magniloquence surrounding her. Theroux demonstrates style is substance: Darconville has it, Isabel hasn't, and 100 pages inside this 700-page novel, the reader knows they have no future, though Darconville won't admit it for hundreds of pages, hoping his powerful imagination can trump unimaginative reality. Darconville's language swells and his rhetorical feats grow more outlandish as he resists that conclusion, resulting in some stunning set-pieces, such as a travelogue of imaginary places and an unholy litany of malevolent women. When he realizes all his imagination and rhetoric still can't change the world, he sickens and dies, right after he finishes penning this work.

It's a pattern Theroux would follow in his two subsequent novels, *An Adultery* (1987) and *Laura Warholic* (2007): a sensitive, overeducated man falls for an insensitive, undereducated woman and suffers as a result. But neither reaches the linguistic heights of *Darconville's Cat*, nor matches its range of registers, from whimsy to intellection, from broad satire to targeted social criticism. Out of print for years, it deserves to be tracked down by any reader interested in love, language, and the complex relationship between the two.

Camilo José Cela — Mrs. Caldwell Speaks to Her Son [1982]

ROSALYN DREXLER

SPEAKING TO BROTHER ABOUT HIS ARTIST FRIEND

Dearest* — you remember that bathtub in the kitchen — your artist friend's? Painted blue. So colorful. Artists are colorful unless they decide on no color at all. You my dear could always project any color that was needed. You'd glow red when warmth was necessary — turn green to cool things down. How do I know this? You told me — and actually when in your presence I could feel the temperature changing. Once I was in a sweat without knowing why. Even in childhood these sweats without fever would appear. Mother called me her little rivulet. I begged you to stop staring at me. When the lights went out, you did. In the dark there was no need for staring — you managed to find your way to me. As for your friend's bathtub in the kitchen — one would think it a decorator's scheme, but no, it was the most expedient thing for a small flat. Pretty colored towels and wash-cloths hung along the edges — tubes of creams and shampoos on each side of the water spigots — whatever was needed for personal hygiene close-by — a most ordinary and useful arrangement. Books for reading while in the bath were placed on a small table in front of the curtained windows — or were the curtains actually a pair of poorly hung brown velvet drapes? On each side of the sink, squares of vigorously scrubbed wood had been cleared. The dishes all white except for one cup from China decorated with blue sampans — and above the sink your friend's watercolors and sketches

---

* Dearest (I dare not pronounce your name).

for larger works. How well you described them to me.

Did you buy him that blue plaid robe hung from a peg on the wall? Did you supply him with the cologne on his dresser? It has a lovely silver top — shining — tightly screwed on to prevent evaporation I suppose, or a nervous habit making sure it was on.

I know that he loved Seurat: the splatter of paint and the awful smell of it. You told me that he lent you a book of reproductions of paintings by Belathquez*. One painting in particular pleased you; the painter painting himself, a mirror trick you said.

You wanted to be an artist yourself but could only get as far as the studio of another artist. Close enough? I think not. Desire tossed carelessly away like a dirty old sock is never found again. The sock hardens and is hurriedly gotten rid of. Once a valuable Patek Philippe watch hidden in a sock was thrown out by you. Couldn't you feel it lying there? You could have saved it. You stupid clean-up man.

I treasure your early drawings: a smiling child in front of a house with all the shades drawn — a dark little bird sitting on the branch of a leafless tree. You said that sorrow knows no season. Is that why the tree had no leaves in summertime?

Can you see me? I'm having a glass of Pinot Grigio* in your honor. I intend to empty the bottle. My forte is staggering from one end of the room to the other — bouncing off the walls — passing out prone on the floor — sleeping a dreamless sleep that foretells the future.

How could you have stayed with that man for so long? That moth-eaten relic wiping his brushes on rotted curtains! Painting ephemeral screaming men seated in plastic boxes is bad enough — but he left it all to you. To you his dutiful companion dedicated to getting him home from the bars night after night. What were you to do with such a legacy? You blew your nose, wiped the tears from your eyes, and left things the way they were for posterity. What a nice man you were. And then you went and died for nothing. They laid you on his bed that was covered with a deep pink quilt: your corpse splattered with vermilion —

---

* Belathquez is the correct pronunciation for Velasquez.
* Pino Grijo is the correct pronunciation for Pinot Grigio.

your skin purple and white — grapes and strawberries — dessert — deserted.

The marks on my upper arm have not gone away. You pressed so hard it hurt me — but you would not let me go. You wanted me to watch as the maggots destroyed you. You needed a witness.

NO MATTER — I SAW NOTHING

D. Keith Mano — Take Five [1982]

NATHAN GADDIS

I first encountered the name D. Keith Mano in Steven Moore's review of *Infinite Jest*. His novel *Take Five* was listed with a dozen fat long novels Moore called "encyclopedic". This fan of *Infinite Jest* was sold ; I jotted down that list and went shopping. For several years. Mano's book —not *Take Five* , not any—was not to be found on any shelf of any bookshop anywhere. I was further intrigued. I broke down and purchased a signed—"For Miriam Berkley—Who had an intimate relationship with me on the Joe Franklin. Best Wishes, D. Keith Mano" (a friend's (secondhand) copy is inscribed, "One of the 11—maybe 12—people to have read <u>Take Five</u>, your name will be etched on a bronze plaque beside my tombstone")—hardcover first edition from a very kind internet bookseller. By this time I had already located and read his penultimate novel *Topless* (the leavings of a Playboy article Mano had been researching) and *War is Heaven!*, his third. I've managed since to locate, purchase, read all nine (alas, only!) Mano novels.

Who is D. Keith Mano? We don't know. For many years he wrote The Gimlet Eye column for the National Review. He wrote countless essays for Playboy, Forbes, etc (over a million words I believe he's claimed) which have not been, and perhaps deserve to be, collected. From 1968 to 1973 he published a novel per year :: *Bishop's Progress, Horn, War is Heaven, The Death and Life of Harry Goth, The Proselytizer,* and *The Bridge*. All out of print today and entirely unknown. For the next several years he set about writing one of the better novels of the later part of the twentieth century, only to have it, naturally, disappear almost about the time it was published, anno domini 1982 (the Dalkey Archive paperback (1998) is possibly still in print). His last mainstream novel, *Topless*, published in 1991, is also..... *The Fergus Dialogues: A Meditation on the*

Gender of Christ (1998), his final novel, is kept in print by a small academic press.

What makes Mano noteworthy? For the simple matter of authorial orientation, he is one of the few, the very few, conservative and christian fictioneers of note from the past half century plus ; perhaps part cause of his being out of print. But really it's just this simple : What makes D. Keith Mano noteworthy is that he wrote *Take Five*. Listen. *Take Five* is not only fantastic on its surface (plot, character, etc), but Mano once revealed what was under its hood and you see maybe, well, listen. Aside from the thing being all about the number Five (how many can you catch?) it was written in iambic pentameter converted to prose, and and and there was this law against repetition that between a whole list of words like "a, to, for, of, until, since, before, unless, in, on" etc or between conjunctions or words with certain suffixes like "-ed, -ing, -ly, -tion, -ous" etc or final 's' at least ten words had to intervene ("You could get spiritual phlebitis gerrymandering all that" says Mano). Needless to say I've not Take Five'd this short note—the question only remaining, was Mano faithful to his schema of restraint? I see three signed first edition copies at abebooks ; let us know!

Thomas Bernhard — Woodcutters [1984]

ANONYMOUS

As I sat on the plastic chair, observing the nouveau riche smugness of the Cauldwell Parent-Teacher Association, I wondered whether the new laws on child discipline would trounce their liberal manners and turn them into proper Cauldwellian bratwhelpers like the authentic residents of this village—the salt-and-grit-eating founders whose efforts in oil and coalmining paved the way for its bourgeois elevation—and bring about a change in the loathsome precocious behaviours I have seen in this region over the last nine months. As I sat on the plastic chair, I contemplated the effrontery of Jill Hampstead's arrogant daughter Mhairi (an inappropriate Highland affectation) as she skipped door-to-door canvassing for the Green Party, patronising adults about their carbon footprints and their failure to use the new green recycling receptacles for wasted foodstuffs, lecturing us on the importance of using public transport over taking our cars to work (I work in a forest where no buses run—does she expect me to walk nine miles every morning?), and other smirk-ridden policies omitting the importance of not having parents who build extensions for their extensions and gazebos in their gazebos (metagazebos, for fuck's sake), and who invest in companies like Shell to fund their precious daughter's Cambridge education. As I sat on the plastic chair, I thought how the parliament's reintroduction of physical punishment for failure to please the teacher would help correct the liberal namby-pambiness that has been eating into our society, and how satisfying it'd be to see a right-hook delivered to Arnold Wilson's brat Daniel's self-loving face as he reels off another word-perfect quote from Chaucer, or to see Laura Marshall's kid Chloe break down when the iron fist is raised during one of her long and tedious Chopin recitals. As I sat on the plastic chair, I thought how my own son Paul might benefit from a classroom ruled in constant terror of a spontaneous ring-fingered thumping—as with the tense dinners I make him endure, where an incorrect word might lead to a violent paternal uprising and a plate of warm spaghetti bolognaise arcing through the air and landing on his head; where an improper term of address might lead to his wind-up radio privileges being revoked for several weeks; where the prospect of him attending university is never even discussed, and the assumption that his future is honest toil on an oil rig or building site is made clear. As I sat on the plastic chair, I decided to make a statement about the new changes as the wine was swirled around their glasses, to deliver a powerful oration laced with backhanded pokes at their insufferable brats, to stand up for the new pro-assault legislation, to make my way towards the front of the room, but the whisky had rendered my legs ineffective, so I had to remain silently brooding in the plastic chair until my wife arrived to pick me up, which took another hour or so, a lateness for which my son would pay dearly.

Christine Brooke-Rose — Amalgamemnon [1984]

ELLEN G. FRIEDMAN

My interest in Christine Brooke-Rose's writing began while editing *Breaking the Sequence: Women's Experimental Fiction* with Miriam Fuchs. No such category as "experimental women writers" had previously been delineated and in our 50-page introduction we presented three generations of such writers, describing them from a feminist point of view. Before we published this volume, feminist literary criticism focused largely on the biographical revelations hidden in the woman writer's experiments. Thus Gertrude Stein's innovations were often explained as aiming to disguise her lesbianism. We were more interested in how women writers' articulated their formal experiments as a space for women's experiences. At the time, we were very much taken with, among others, Hélène Cixous' theory of *l'écriture féminine*. The flaw in this idea, particularly in Cixous, was the divorce from signature, so that both men and women, she argued, could write the feminine. Her examples, in fact, came mainly from male writers. James Joyce she argued, wrote *l'écriture féminine*. In contrast, we saw a multi-generational tradition of women writers who experimented with narrative forms to express elements of their gender not fully allowed in traditional modes.

We opened our volume with an essay Christine Brooke-Rose wrote for us entitled 'Illiterations'. In this essay she writes directly of the canon as a "male preserve" from which women as a class have been prohibited:

> In theory the canonic/non-canonic opposition applies to all writers and thus cuts across sexual and any other oppositions. In practice a canon is very much a masculine notion, a priesthood (not to be polluted by women), a club, a sacred male pre-

serve....

[Thus] this notion of a canon, of a central tradition around the central myth, which is essentially male, priestly and caste-bound, underlies types and levels of critical attention, so that despite the various and increasing waves of emancipation since the 19th century, certain relics remain, ill iterations in the unconscious of society.

Just as 'Illiterations' is a clear-headed and smart explanation, *Amalgamemnon* is brilliantly evocative of Brooke-Rose's feminism—though she resisted this label. In this first-person narrative, all men are versions of Agamemnon (hence, 'Amalgamemnon') and all women Cassandra. The linguistic wit and formal risks are so brilliant and elegant as they illuminate feminist insights that the text was a revelation to me. *Amalgamemnon* is still my favorite of her texts. I laugh out loud even now as I think about how Agamemnon is torn to pieces and then reassembled as a contemporary lover named variously Willy and Wally, an incarnation in which his general authority has been atomized.

When she resurrects the mythical and historical in the contemporary, they lose what Walter Benjamin called their "aura", and we can see them clearly. For instance, she ties the conventional wisdom that "No young woman would allow herself to be abducted [read 'raped'] without in fact wishing to be" as a legacy of the stories of Helen and Cassandra, among others, as transmitted by Homer and other literary fathers whose interests lay with the successful abduction. In addition, she presents the relationship between Cassandra and Agamemnon as a trope for the relationship of women to the male establishment generally, a relationship in which women, bearing the legacy of Cassandra, have no credibility or voice.

When the narrator, a professor of literature and history, fears she will be declared "redundant," her language sacrificed to the language of computers, she compares her situation to that of the Amazons. Presenting her observation in the future tense (in which the entire novel is cast), she speculates, "The young Scythians will be unable to learn the language of the Amazons but the women will succeed in picking up theirs, and therefore disappear" (11).

The humor of the wordplay in which Brooke-Rose revelled also drew me in:

> *Tomorrow at breakfast Willy will pleased as punch bring out as the fruit of deep reflection the non-creativity of women look at music painting sculpture in history and I shall put on my postface and mimagree, unless I put on my preface and go through the routine of certain social factors such as disparagement from birth the lack of expectation not to mention facilities a womb of one's own a womb with a view an enormous womb and he won't like the countertone at all, unless his eyes will be sexclaiming still what fun, it'll talk if you wind it up. . . .*

The sobering insights, the depth of her understanding and scholarship, the smart humor and irrepressible wit are reasons enough for this book to interest generations of readers, not to mention her unbounded optimism: "Sooner or later the future will explode into the present despite the double standard at breaking points."

Rikki Ducornet — The Stain [1984]

MICHELLE RYAN-SAUTOUR

A CELEBRATION OF THE GOLDEN HARE

The Stain is an awakening. As I immerse myself in Rikki Ducornet's novel many years after my initial reading, I am once again filled with the odors, sounds, familiar cities, troglodyte houses, superstitions, eccentric characters, a very deep sense of the earth, and a strong attachment to the *terroir* of the Loire Valley. This novel feeds my senses and opens my mind, and I am carried away by the vision of the golden hare at the end of the novel. It is a book of shit, harsh violence, superstitious sacrifices, twisted martyrdom, and playfully perverse sexual frolic, but it is also a foray into the bright magic of existence, as it culminates in a celebration of the deep forces of the imagination. *The Stain* was my first encounter with Rikki Ducornet's writing, and I was thoroughly seduced.

Rikki Ducornet's writing was first brought to my attention by Ben Forkner, a university professor at Université d'Angers, in the Loire Valley. He spoke of her tetralogy of novels based on the four elements, and urged me to read her work, explaining how her writing would gain in recognition. I also live in the Loire Valley, only thirty kilometers from where Rikki Ducornet was living in Le Puy Notre Dame when she wrote *The Stain*. Echoes of familiar villages and landscapes lend a particular intimacy to the imagined world of "La Folie", as they appeal to my inner eye and body. Although she attributes much of this village's "folly" to the inherently surreal quality of small village life in France in the 1960s, I feel as if I know these characters and places, and I am given an acute sense of the peculiar in the familiar. I also feel a close connection with the main character Charlotte, a child whose uniqueness transpires in a hare-shaped birthmark, an image of magical proportions that warms and glows throughout the novel.

Like many of Rikki Ducornet's characters, Charlotte travels the wavering edges of childhood and adulthood. The novel embraces light traces of "Little Red Riding Hood" as Charlotte navigates the changing landscape of her body and the wolves around her. These "wolves" are not only threats to sexuality, but also insidious powers that seek to stifle the life of the mind and senses. Charlotte's engagement with the strictures of Catholicism and the superstitions of French rural village life is fraught with complexity. Oddly, she feeds off of the teeming madness around her, while also moving beyond it, ultimately finding a home with Archange and blossoming into a realm of wonder and creation. One cannot help but find an echo of Rikki Ducornet's own development as an artist and writer. This was her first novel, a work that she says originated in a dream. Judging by the rich collection of works that have followed this first novel, much like Charlotte she has never really woken up from the glow of the golden hare: "He casts a spell from which she will never entirely awaken, not even when the years will have carried her far from this time and place" (189).

Christoph Meckel — The Figure on the Boundary Line [1984]

BEN WINCH

"Night and day I am on the road through landscapes familiar and unknown, seen and imagined."
So wrote Christoph Meckel in 1969 ('Workshop Notes'), and we should take him at his word. Though terse, clipped, humble, intimately concerned with *things*, his prose—in the 1-100 page pieces of these 160 pages—is above all visionary. At first (and this is remarkable, given my former obsession with the topic) I didn't realise: he's a successor to Kafka. Of course in his native German this must be more common, but his method of appropriating the legacy is unique. Without spectacle, without visible effort, in plain, precise language he *takes off* from the platform of 'A Country Doctor', of 'The Vulture', to a place just as elemental, just as natural, and which retains all the warmth of Kafka's own predecessor Robert Walser: no rants here, no spiral staircases, no Chinese-box-within-boxes.

A city, besieged by flood and avalanche, constantly rearranges itself with its multitude of cranes. ('Baan'.)

A man in a ticket-box watches the entrance to a cave, selling maps, charging admission, until people emerge from the cave whom he has never seen. ('My Friends'.)

A housesitter in a plush residence is gradually tempted to the boundary line by a vagrant, eventually following his own life of vagrancy. ('Figure on the Boundary Line'.)

In the novella-centrepiece 'Tullipan'—his *The Robber*, his *Unnamable*—Meckel describes with minute veracity the visitations of an alter-ego, initiating an inquiry into the species of fictional characters as profound as his high-modernist ancestors' but in prose so simple it could soothe a child. (Illustrations by Dick Bruna—of *Miffy at the Seaside*—would not be out of place.)

Is he primitive? postmodern? fabulist?

"It seems that the German public of the last twenty-five years," wrote translator, friend and early Walser-champion Christopher Middleton in 1983, "has tended to prefer astute father-figure writers to incorrigible son-figures like Meckel."

Maybe so, but:

Meckel's art is sophisticated, honed to near-essence, thus can reach/penetrate/resemble the child.

It is timeless, unconcerned with "new", but unique. A forgotten (or in English never-taken) branch of literature perhaps, but durable—alive, green, sturdy. It will long be capable of supporting weight.

It is *journey, exploration*. "Do not suppose for a minute that fiction the way I do it is a simple diversion." ('Inventions'.) And (in 'Workshop Notes'): "there is a bar of fog, an uncrossable edge of the magic world . . ."

Too often (in Bernhard, in Handke) I've felt that fog as confounding, as something through which its explorers daren't penetrate but just describe circles, content to have reached it, to inhabit it. But Meckel, like his "columns of dead" on the march against the wind, presses on: "The wind is the defender of the exits, they shout, we are on the right road!" ('Manifesto of the Dead'.)

If these quiet miniatures are typical of Meckel, his obscurity is expected. He won't raise his voice. Hush, and you'll hear him. The most important discovery—for this reader—since Robert Walser.

Milorad Pavić — *Dictionary of the Khazars* [1984]

ALEC NEVALA-LEE

MALE EDITION

Dictionary of the Khazars comes closer than any novel I know to laying out a series of increasingly improbable formal challenges and succeeding on every level, provided that we encounter it with a corresponding leap of the imagination. As its title implies, Milorad Pavić's work is a dictionary—or, more precisely, three dictionaries with a preface and two appendices—in which the entries can be read in any order. You can plow straight through, or read parallel entries in different sections, or follow the text from one cross-reference to the next. Characters mentioned briefly in one entry receive full treatment in another; you can hear the end of one story before stumbling across its beginning or middle; and throughout, there are teasing hints of a greater pattern visible only to those who absorb the book as a whole.

Remarkably, it delivers, and the effect on the last page, when the full picture locks in place, is shattering and unforgettable. If I react so emotionally to its conclusion, it's in part because of the role this book has played in my own life: I bought a copy before I started college and browsed inside it until I knew certain pages almost by heart, but I finished it only in my thirties. Yet it's also a reflection of Pavic's craft and intelligence. If individual entries are maddeningly enigmatic, the overall structure is ruthlessly logical: at least one crucial entry and the second appendix aren't referenced anywhere else, which subtly ensures that the reader will find them last.

The result is the kind of nonlinear antibook that paradoxically makes the strongest possible case for books as a physical medium, since it allows you to turn pages in both directions, with simultaneous access to all sections at once. The scholar Espen J. Aareseth draws a useful distinction between ergodic works, which place nontrivial demands on the reader in traversing or assembling the text, and their nonergodic counterparts, which ask nothing but "eye movement and the periodic or arbitrary turning of pages." Ergodic fiction constantly alerts you to the strangeness of reading itself, and at its finest, as here or in *Pale Fire*, it implicates you in the process of its own creation, until it seems less like a book than a place you can never entirely escape.

Such stories push against form, but that doesn't mean they want to be liberated: their significance lies in the act of turning pages both ways. (When writing *Infinite Jest*, David Foster Wallace was adamant about using endnotes instead of footnotes, forcing readers to go "literally physically 'back and forth' in a way that perhaps cutely mimics some of the story's thematic concerns.") *Dictionary of the Khazars* would lose much of its power on a tablet or screen, where our familiarity with moving from one link to another would cause its novelty to disappear. Most great works of imagination are already hypertexts: Dante demands to be interpreted both vertically and horizontally, and the reader of *Ulysses* or *Gravity's Rainbow* ends up confronting every page in relation to every other. *Dictionary of the Khazars* takes the experiment to its limit, but like its peers, it achieves full meaning only within the covers that barely contain it.

Milorad Pavić — Dictionary of the Khazars [1984]

SILVIA BARLAAM

FEMALE EDITION

You can buy The Male Edition of this book. Or you can buy The Female Edition. Or if your reading needs are digitally satisfied, you can buy The Androgynous Edition, whereby the significant sixteen different lines are female in the edition and male in its introduction. What a difference. And yet, a world. Where everything—people, facts, legends—has more than one version, more than one witness, more than one critical expert commentary, and the male and female principles run circles around each other, walk in other people's dreams, never meeting if not at the end of the book in the author's own words, hopefully a male and female reader who can make meaning of it all, together. But in this lies the brilliance of a book wherein each element does not live on its own, doesn't have one identity, one truth, but shows a different trait according to whom is doing the looking/reading.

Reconstructions and revisions float across the pages in silent clamour for attention, but in its essence, the book's narrative is only complete when both versions are read.

Dictionary of the Female Version of the Dictionary of the Khazars

thumb: a fundamental symbolic human appendage that appears in bi-thumbed Khazars icons, it expresses principles and connections and unity and the two sides of the same coin. A legend tells of *The Thumb that Got Lost* and in female dreams it found a map to its road home, a land where past and future are multi-thumbed and trembling when they touch.

feelings: a locality of imponderability, where many lost trains of thought reside permanently.

centuries: a type of measurement for lines of text, however the quantities are expressed in unfathomable states of mind where one—especially female readers—loses contact with their aware mind but gains invaluable insights in the meaning of life. Or of narrative.

text: an assemblage of signs of often indecipherable interpretation, always dubious intentions and forever fascinating aesthetics. In some instances, dark-inked versions of texts have been seen through translucent mirrors as many thumbed hands were grasping at them, folio pages skilfully mashed catching them on the adversary winds.

reader: never one or the same, changed by the lexical experiences unwillingly acquired in dreams often dreamed by others, frequently cautioned and guided in the reading experience by knowledgeable words in forewords or afterwords, but not necessarily a follower of said words, and certainly the wiser for not licking their fingers after thumbing potentially poisoned pages. The particular reader in the Female Edition of the *Dictionary of the Khazars* is understood as that specific type of reader which can choose not to read at all.

Also, see: **you**.

Don Delillo — White Noise [1985]

BARBARA MELVILLE

White Noise by Don DeLillo made me cry. Let me be clear about this —I'm not a sentimental book-crying person. I don't even hang out with people like that. So my reaction had to be down to Tortured Artist Syndrome. A belligerent head voice, which sounded like my dad spliced with my first boss, was telling me I'd never write with the wisdom and astuteness of Don DeLillo. At best, they explained, I'd keep trying to replicate his subtle aphoristic sentences, and one day, I might stumble into some half-arsed parallel universe where reviewers say *good grief, she thinks she's Don DeLillo*. But I'd best warn you now—that day isn't even near. This essay isn't positive and it isn't going anywhere profound. It's just going to stop at some point, and so are you.

So, my stereotypical artistic tendencies weren't what caused my tears. I realised this a few years later while travelling in the Arctic Circle. It was the middle of the night and I was sitting on a hill in Lapland, surrounded by perfect sunshine. I should have felt any number of negative emotions involving sentences I wished to write but couldn't. Instead I felt peace. The 24-hour sun melted away the constant tick of time. Clocks didn't move forward or back, they just didn't move. As I watched the skies, a moment from *White Noise* popped into my head. In its final pages, Jack tells us of how he and his wife Babette watch the sunset together. But his descriptions are not borne of connection, warmth or epiphany. Sunsets, we learn, are death knells. The more sunsets we collect, the closer we get to the inevitable ends of our molecules, our selves, our lives.

I had cried because I was scared. On reading that final page I internalised the loss of the person I love most in the world: me. My future self, even if she isn't perfect, and even if she can't write the sentences she wants to, is on the clock. This fear of death creeps into the roots of everything we do. It has to. Some of us have to be good in life or we won't gain entry to the heaven of our dreams. Others like me have to counter our atheist predictions of nothingness with a meaningful stint on earth. Every mouthful of food and laugh of joy is about giving our lives and bodies that meaning. The children or books we bear are our legacies, where we trick ourselves into thinking that being remembered is somehow enough.

But it isn't enough. Babette had the cure for the fear of death: a sinister drug called Dylar. But it wasn't really a cure. The fear was always there underneath, and in reality, there is nothing so readily bottled. So on the way home from Lapland, I was bereft, grieving the peace I had experienced. I went through London: the antithesis of timelessness. Precious seconds were slipping away faster than usual. The time I had saved was being lost. How could I get it back? How could I feel that peace again? When I finally got home to Edinburgh, I got as close as I could to Lapland, to Dylar. I tore up the calendars. I shut the curtains on sunsets for good. Then I smashed every clock I could find. That was a few months ago now, and I'm still waiting. I'll let you know when it works.

Gilbert Sorrentino — Pack of Lies [1985-1989]

DICK WITHERSPOON

Have you read Leo Kaufman's *Isolate Flecks*?
    Forgive me if I say this is a ridiculous question?   No one has read that hack   I mean you know that idea was stolen from another writer   yes yes Sorenti   Italian-American please   I wouldn't use that word   obsessed with structures   hidden ones   the sort that aren't obvious   like beginning middle and end   a basic example Mrs Henry's panties?   what does that have to do with
    yes yes form generates content   heard that one before
    please don't interrupt with basic observations   have you read *Strange Letter*   yes deliberately obfuscating   not too large a word   a multitude of voices telling different versions of events   multitude is not a word Miss Lorpailleur might use
    what voices?   depends who is talking   ha ha   who am I? not the same person who started this response that's for sure
    no I have not read *La Bouche métallique*   utter filth   did you hear what they said about *Isolate Flecks*?   back to *Strange Letter* yes
    it's a detective story   where you never know what crime was committed   or who committed the crime   yes that is a brilliant idea Miss Ostrom?   she has nothing to do with Sorenti
    apart from the former marriage   that's in the past
    and how about *Tulip Cinema*   takes the women from *Strange Letter*   the female characters   that is not reductivist
    have you been speaking to Miss Butler again   damn feminist brigade   that is not offensive   dammit   it is structured around props from the old English Tulip cinema   the con-

tent is formed based on what is evoked from each prop
    Leo stole this idea for his novel   at least that's what April Detective said   she's the one who ahem   with Lou at the party   what do you mean what party?   what have we been discussing here   *Mysteriousa*   yes the final novel in the trilogy
    Leo is in there as Liff Koffmal   author of *Ironize Flicks* yes not very subtle   *Hellions in Hosiery?*   of course I read that novel   I co-wrote that with   back to Sorrento   yes I mean Sorenti apologies   he went through the two preceding books and made a list of the proper nouns   for *Mysteriousa* yes   and linked alphabetically all the nouns he listed to generate the content yes
    what do you mean why can't he write a proper novel like Antony Lamont's *Guinea Red*   love that book   I helped with the re-write   so these novels   exhilarating and challenging
    maddening perhaps   hilarious too   a fine example of some of the most innovative exploratory writing from America   all right *the world* then   I don't aim to localise   on a par with Beckett's trilogy?   why not   it's not for me to dispense hyperbole   yes I believe Miss Ostrom had a copy at the party
    she was reading aloud to Leo   he had a pained expression
    Sorenti appeared for a few minutes   spoke to April I believe they exited in her car mint-green Chevrolet   I fail to see the significance   she did release a novel a month later   what are you implying

Ronald Sukenick — In Form: Digressions on the Act of Fiction [1985]

TOM WILLARD

DEAD LETTERS

"Is there anything that is not narrative?"— Gertrude Stein

I was once informed while working at Starbucks corporate, "you used to have to be disciple of the bean to work for Starbucks, now they will just hire anyone." Aghast, I glanced around at the posters stapled to the cheap cubicle walls alerting us to the precise number of additional hours customers waited on hold due to our wanton indifference toward the concept of being punctual. At some point in my brief tenure I received a voicemail from the CEO urging all "partners" to discover a new found passion for the bean, yes a coffee bean. Frequently, my melancholic colleagues share another tale of woe: "all I want is a job I feel passionate about, I just don't feel passionate about this." While the rhetoric sounds as if I am reporting from the USSR in 1936, rest assured, we are safely in 21st century America. Once the world offered a limitless horizon promising adventure and myth, but has now been reduced to a Kafkan nightmare where one should feel passionate about completing bureaucratic tasks in front of the dull gray glow of a computer monitor. How have we arrived at a world where passion has been reduced from Dante's poetic longing toward Beatrice to creating a php script that writes user information to a database? Can a lone Surfictionist named Ronald Sukenick liberate language from corporate colonisation, freeing language from these preconceived formulations?

While some elements of contemporary corporate culture may have eluded Sukenick when he wrote the essays that comprise *In Form: Digressions on the Act of Fiction*, he prophetically tried to liberate thought and language from its seductive embrace. Sukenick demands that we release all thought from ideological ends and from all service, as he is skeptical of motives: "The pressure of the mass media (corporate America), which is nothing so much as the manipulation of the mass imagination, a sellout of individual experience. The media imposes manipulative paradigms on individual experience." Whose interests are we being manipulated to fulfill? The interests of corporations, Wall Street, and politicians insist we maintain a certain set of relations that facilitate the production and sales of goods. Sukenick urges us to escape this premeditated reality, to deconstruct the construct. But how?

How do we release language from the service or a particular order or construct? Sukenick offers us two complementary strategies: to create narratives that capture the form of consciousness as it freely interacts with the world and language games that include puns, wordplay, collage, and montage. The latter creates the conditions for the former, which in turn creates the possibility to "defamiliarize and destabilize the conventional view of reality", revealing new possibilities for experience.

The form of fiction that best represents the crass manipulation of experience is realism; it's also what Sukenick's aesthetics hope to subvert. Realist aesthetics reinforce the static meanings that inform the power relations that benefit the 1%. Language games, puns, and wordplay open new spaces within language that release "the possibility of meaning that is inherent in language." Sukenick's strategy represents a literature of liberation that can free us from the manipulative "disciples of the bean", breathing new life into the dead letters of the present.

Marcel Bénabou — Why I Have Not Written Any of My Books [1986]

A. WRITER

THE INSPIRED POST-ITS OF WRITER AARON J. SIMPSON

> A post-apocalyptic noir set in the Sears tower (top floor—post-flood civilisation). Romantic or brutal? > Hector is a cosmetics salesman who finds himself allergic to the products he peddles. Could an attempt to woo a desired customer lead to certain death? Anti-consumerist parable. > WRITE ABOUT YOUR BREAKUP!!! > Comic novel about a leper colony, a student is thrown in there by accident, becomes a leper. Touching identification with lepers and overcomes bigotry, etc. > A novel with twenty-six narrators, each identifiable through use of their alphabetical referents. Similar to Perec—narrators (i.e. letters) disappear from language? too similar to *Ella Minnow Pea*?—message about corruption, misuse of language—too didactic? > An attempt to exhaust a car park in Bognor Regis. > A short, understated book on litotes. > Star Wars and the Holocaust—links? > A man eats a pen cap and forgets. Five decades later the pen cap emerges at stool. (800 pages?) > Gimps and chimps (and pimps?) > WRITE SOMETHING ON THE SCHOOL MASSACRE!!! > A detective tale with no murderer, no crime, and no detective. The implication of wrongdoing. (Nine-book series?) > A novel comprised of ideas for novels (or the first page of novels?), possible Calvino or Chitarroni ripoff. > Narrator is critic. Each chapter contains venom against a chosen hated novel. Might seem anti-literature. A two-volume set? Other volume praising novels? > Peter Redgrove meets The Vaselines at a Puccini recital. > An acrostic novel where the acrostic

spells out a poisonous ideology—a symbol of the importance of close reading in the digital age? > A crime novel set in a locked shed (a series of "locked shed" mysteries?) > *Oliver Twist* set in a Chinese child labour camp—capitalist satire? > WRITE ABOUT DEATH!!! > A walrus swallows its tusks and whiskers—a metaphor. > A rewrite of Gore Vidal's *Duluth* omitting the nouns. > A serious account of the Arab Spring with baffling-but-hilarious anti-Islam jokes as footnotes? > A fake exegesis of *Finnegans Wake*—what for?! > Aaron J. Simpson awakes to the news someone with the same name has published the same book he was working on. References to Gogol and Dostoevsky. > Finish (start) thesis on Raymond Queneau. > A novel about a failed attempt to start a thesis on Raymond Queneau? > Self-publish chapbook of erotic haiku about Holly Hunter?—pen name Max Danger? > Narrator who meditates on the songs of Elvis Costello, Seneca's *The Apocolocyntosis*, and the movies of Gregg Araki. > Is my prose blue, red, or green? > The shopping list as a literary form? what does this mean?? > Simple story about a broken-hearted man? > WRITE ABOUT LOVE!!! > A novel about a man too overwhelmed by the innumerable novels about love to write another one, decides he's better off writing one about Nebraskan sheep farming (in Latin!) > A cultural history of the golliwog. > From POV of a raindrop. Sun as villain. > Novel in Latin about Nebraskan sheep farming.

Michael Westlake — Imaginary Women [1987]

MICHAEL WESTLAKE

Like most of my fiction, *Imaginary Women* stemmed from a particular life situation in a specific place, and the confluence of the various concerns and points of fascination that were important to me at the time. Thus "our city", although never named, bears an oneiric resemblance to Manchester, subject to the condensations, displacements, distortions and random associations of the dreamwork. Its Chihuahua Club, the site of the conflict between two women of means—The General and La Jefe—and their dogs Puch and Pique, offers its all-women clientele copies of Pravda and the Wall Street Journal, but no Manchester Evening News. The "the hills to the east of our city", where the independent filmmaker Mac**ash—candidate letters for the asterisks successively irrupt and are superseded—heads after the outcry on the release of her film *Pork* and where Clemency goes potholing and discovers three flights of thirteen steps cut into the rock, are a simulacrum of the Pennines. The library where the revolutionary librarian P. Birdwissel turns the existed order upside down Mancunians may misrecognize as the Central Reference Library. An imaginary Manchester for its imaginary women.

An occasional storyline is narrated by Adolphus/Amadeus/Augustus, Mac**ash's cat, opening with three noirish villains, possibly identifiable from the *The Maltese Falcon*, arriving at the "Fur Q vehicle", Mac**ash's home and working environment. Psychoanalytic mayhem ensues, requiring the aleatory intervention of numerous women and the odd man or two to restore the dismembered patriarchal order in a putatively matriarchal modality. Signifiers abound in this impossible quest:

Chinese ideograms, Matisse paintings, snooker ball layouts, restitutive tattooing, poker hands, mathematical figures, the repeated stammered f-f-f redolent of Evelyn Mulwray's my f-f-father in *Chinatown* . . . *Imaginary Women* is far from linear.

The assemblage of the various "steps"—three flights of thirteen—into the pre-planned algorithmic structure took place in a south Manchester pub in the company of my friend the late Antony Easthope—who wrote about *IW* in his *British Poststructuralism*. At the time I was unaware of Oulipo, the existence of which I only discovered later, in Paris, through meeting Harry Mathews, a close friend of Georges Perec. It turned out that Mathews and I, as well as Christine Brooke-Rose, whose work I was already familiar with, shared the same Manchester publisher, the redoutable Carcanet Press. While my own use of arbitrary constraints to channel my thinking involved larger textual units than Oulipo's micro-constraints—most strikingly Perec's e-less novel *La Disparition*—it was interesting to find that I had independently been working along similar lines. Subsequently I developed and refined this approach, as in the overdetermining frameworks of *51 Soko* and *The Triumph of Love and Other Paintings*. Like *IW*, these were attempts to elaborate formal structures able to articulate what would otherwise remain unwritten or even unwritable. Not formalism for its own sake—though I have nothing against that—but formalism as a way of courting the necessarily elusive real.

Nicholson Baker — *The Mezzanine* [1988]

M.J. NICHOLLS

Whenever I board a train I look for the seat farthest from other passengers as possible. To read, I need silence, or near silence—I need at least five or six seats distance. Finding the right seat is an exact science. One night, coming home from a concert, I enter the car and there are people spread at an infuriating equidistance apart, almost positioned on purpose at four-seat spaces to upset the four-to-six space rule. I walk past the menacing night-people, who are all potential murders and rapists until proven otherwise, and locate a seat in the left row between two solo passengers, with a space of about three seats in front and two seats behind and another man two seats ahead in the right row. A trio of women conduct a conversation up ahead, their voices muted at first but rising from time to time, competing with the rattle of the moving train. This is the strongest threat to an undisturbed reading of Baker. *The Mezzanine* requires concentration and is not trainfodder. The protagonist discusses the exaggerated minutiae of certain trivial aspects of his life, from shoelaces to escalator etiquette, to the value of paper towels over hand driers, each topic accumulating an absurd level of detail with laughter as the release. I read for a few moments and a loud titter interrupts. These are not the sober revellers I had assumed in that micro-second of noticing. These women are about to embark on a drunken confab punctuated with shrieks and whoops. I fight. I keep reading. I am unable to mute their drivel about some bloke being a dick and someone needing to phone someone and tell him something about being a dick or something because he shouldn't have said that, whoever he is, this traitorous dick. There are further dilem-

137

mas. I am short-sighted with a slight squint, and the lights on Scotrail trains are diffuse and dim. Reading the footnotes becomes a chore for me, trying to follow these complex tangents in the Granta edition's petite font under appalling lights, and the darkness outside offers no help. I can't bring the book right up close, as this can affect my long-range vision. If I am focusing on focusing my eyes, I'll stop focusing my brain—reading and not taking in the words. I wait until the women leave. At the next stop, the paranoia that a lunatic has boarded the train and wants to kill me becomes so intense, I have to look up and make a quick assessment of the new passenger, check his psycho credentials. If he sits behind me, which he does, I will have to keep one hand on my possessions, in case he should slide a hand through the half-inch seat space and steal my valuables. I am alone in the train with a psycho behind me. Paranoia increases as I contemplate the horrors of being robbed or stabbed. I picture a pocket knife being poked into my ribs, a wire being stretched across my neck. There's no point reading now, not with death on the cards. I become dour, thinking about other problems—financial, personal, familial—making each problem into something huge and insurmountable, until I can't stand to even hold the book, so depressed and self-involved have I become in those four minutes. I have read almost half a page.

Italo Calvino — Six Memos for the Next Millennium [1988]

DANIEL LEVIN BECKER

The first thing even an amateur literary sleuth will notice about *Six Memos for the Next Millennium* (tr. Patrick Creagh) is that it contains only five memos. The sixth, which was to be on the theme of consistency—each memo is a lecture Calvino wrote to deliver at Harvard between 1985 and 1986, taking as its subject one of the "values, qualities, or peculiarities" of literature—was unwritten when Calvino died in Italy of a cerebral hemorrhage. His widow, Esther, tells us he had planned to write it in Cambridge, unlike the first five. Consistency indeed.

But *Six Memos* is not much of a work for the literary sleuth, not the way some of Calvino's fiction is, particularly the mischievously spectacular productions of his later years. It is rather an occasion for him to share with us the preoccupations and discoveries of a tirelessly agile mind, the side of it that belonged to the reader and not the writer—or, if you like, to the literary sleuth and not the diabolical genius. "In this talk," he says at the beginning of the first lecture, on the theme of lightness, "I shall try to explain—both to myself and to you—why I have come to consider lightness a value rather than a defect."

The end of that statement (which is actually broken off at a semicolon, but I have a word limit) is of value, certainly, as are the initiatory questions and theories underpinning each of the other memos, and the provisional answers at which Calvino arrives. What makes the book for me, though, is in that aside between the dashes, the earnest and generous spirit of inquiry into which we would-be listeners are invited: it is not just for our benefit that he picks his way among literary touchstones small and large, near and far, old and new, universal and particular, but for his own too.

And, more than his gestures toward conclusive insight, it is the dawdling rhythm of his path that has stuck with me since I marked up my first copy so effusively that I would later refuse to lend it to a love interest: not the meaning of exactitude, say, so much as the anecdotes he picks up to dust off and admire while traveling in its jurisdiction. These tend to lodge so stubbornly in my brain that I sometimes mistake their source for my own readerly travels, not Calvino's: the draftsman and the crab, the detective and his perpetually half-smoked cigarette, Monterroso and the dinosaur.

Or for that matter the emperor in love with the lake—more precisely, upon revisiting the *Memos*, Charlemagne in love with Lake Constance. Consistency indeed after all, at least in the wealth of mystery and magic and cosmicomic benediction that touches all things Calvinian: the same command of serendipity and reflexivity he shows off when he remarks, of Georges Perec's *Life A User's Manual*, that "this ultra-completed book has an intentional loophole left for incompleteness." Well played, old man.

David Markson — Wittgenstein's Mistress [1988]

CHRISTOPHER WUNDERLEE

David Markson's *Wittgenstein's Mistress* is about a solitary exchange and what that means to the limitations of language. I read it as a sort of dialogue between THE Wittgenstein and the one and only Samuel Beckett. THE Wittgenstein spent his early energies focused on how language fails to accurately capture reality. The one and only Samuel Beckett didn't believe in reality—he really didn't.

Beckett placed figures in unnamed, unsure environments without the cloak of religion. Markson placed Kate in *Wittgenstein's Mistress* as supposedly the last person on earth in the Metropolitan Museum (she calls herself the "curator of all the world"). Markson's setting is as unnamed and unsure of an environment—it becomes apparent that Kate has a way of defining a truth and then deconstructing as a way of making it more true.

Kate offers forth THE Wittgenstein-style musings about a range of topics. "If there were no more copies accessible anywhere of 'Anna Karenina' . . . would its title still be 'Anna Karenina'?" and "Where was the poster when it was on the wall in my head but was not on the wall in the other house?"

We learn Kate has been alone for 10 years; however, just as soon, she begins qualifying this 'history'. "And none of what I have just written having been what really happened in either event".

It's as if THE Wittgenstein says something profound and the one and only Samuel Beckett responds and then it switches or one interrupts the other or one goes off for a while. Thus, Kate's monologue (both authors were specialists) becomes a philosophical dialectic between two systems—one correcting the other.

The two systems are accentuated by the structure of the novel—the Beckettian setting and Wittgensteinesque narration. Although it is titled *Wittgenstein's Mistress*, not Beckett's Paramour.

Beckett's paramour would have been, 'our vulgar perception', which he said in an essay on Proust, 'is not concerned with other than vulgar phenomena'. Beckett's paramour's 'vulgar phenomena' originates from, 'the world being a projection of the individual's consciousness'.

Wittgenstein's Mistress is a lonely (possibly insane) woman named Kate whose statements are meaningful because they can be defined and pictured and thus, they represent a reality.

Kate tells us, "I am not particularly happy over this new habit of saying things that I have very little idea what I mean by saying, to tell the truth". Her 'odd couple' dialogue challenges THE Wittgenstein and the one and only Beckett. In fact, Kate challenges just about every philosophical or aesthetic system throughout the book, and she does so by allowing revisionism to conquer what first appears to be the truth.

The truth is apparent in what she first explains; however, she soon deconstructs this truth. "I still notice the burned house, mornings, when I walk along the beach . . . Well, obviously I do not notice the house. What I notice is what remains of the house."

In *Wittgenstein's Mistress*, we notice the burned house at first but then we realize we aren't noticing the burned house . . . what we're noticing is what remains.

Janice Galloway — The Trick is to Keep Breathing [1989]

GILLIAN DEVINE

The Trick is to Keep Breathing is a fragmented and revealing insight into the mind of a young woman, and reluctant narrator, who does not want to let you know how she is really thinking or feeling, putting a brave face on everything.

The narration is consistently dispassionate, simply observing and describing everything in her "average day" as she goes along. Signs materialize out of nowhere, giving no real indication of where she is, or is going—lists offering more of a sign of the order in which she tries to keep everything. She doesn't even want to let you know her real name, only later on revealing it as Joy, or Miss Stone.

Clues begin to creep in that she is troubled deep down. A mural she sees in passing is described as having a traditional family with a "snake-green lawn", and the way the words are written often resemble a thought process, non-linear but far more revealing of how she's really feeling. The first interaction in the story comes from a health visitor, which is the first external "evidence" that she is suffering from an unspecified condition, the nature of which we can only glean from more clues further on.

Dissociation pervades the narrative. Being in crowds makes Joy "depressed . . . As though I'm trapped in a coop full of hens for the slaughterhouse." When she does talk to other people, the conversations read almost—in one case exactly—like a script, showing that she sees herself as simply performing a role which she has to keep on playing. Her best friend is away on holiday for the duration of the story, sending by post her own fragments of a lifestyle which Joy can only imagine from a distance.

The first full "conversation" has only one side, when she settles down to read a magazine, and the horoscopes and advice columns and articles all promise something which Joy somehow feels she doesn't deserve.

She begins to have flashbacks, which initially seem vague and detached, as if they are fragments of a dream, but soon it becomes more obvious that they are flashbacks of memories, and of one in particular, which contains a past tragedy. Some time ago, she had begun an affair with a married man, and from the flashbacks that continue throughout the story, she really did love him and was loved in return. One dark day, he drowned on holiday and, retrospectively, we can see how Joy was once a happy and life-loving young woman, and one who, if anything, followed her heart to a fault, finding the love she wanted and needed in the wrong place, yet placing no blame when the tragic ending came.

Yet somehow she pushes on with the "play", finding her way to a place where she is perhaps not quite happy, but can keep going on with her life, with the implication that maybe one day, if she's lucky, happiness will follow on its own.

Janice Galloway has a way of putting thoughts and feeling down on the page which are far more telling than doing so in the "conventional way", which show the confusion which the narrator often feels when they see themselves as being separate from everyone else. *The Trick is to Keep Breathing* walks the person reading, in the narrator's own way, through the precise nature of the things they have to do just to keep going.

Jacques Roubaud — The Great Fire of London [1989]

IAN MONK

Known primarily in his native France as a poet, Jacques Roubaud, the prolific writer, mathematician, polymath and the first person to be co-opted to the Oulipo after the generation of founders, is also the author of several novels and other prose works, in particular his *magnum opus* 'Le grand incendie de Londres', which runs to six large volumes (or 'branches'). The bad news is that only the first three have so far been translated into English (to declare my interest, the third by this writer). The good news is that the fourth is in preparation (by another translator) and the others will no doubt follow, as Dalkey Archive intends to publish the entire work.

Written in the early hours of each morning over several years, the work is an early example of the sort of protocol-based writing that has interested the Oulipo more and more in recent years: the writer has to proceed by memory-based glimpses of the past, written in short, numbered sections composed day by day, and he can only continue his narrative once each memory/image has been fully grasped and crystallised; he is not allowed to go back and 'correct' what has already been written, and so must press onwards with the text, no matter what. Meanwhile, the direction of Roubaud's main narrative is constantly broken and interrupted by a series of interpolations, which vary from short parentheses to long 'bifurcations' occupying several sections, across many pages. Miraculously, the author's sure hand and limpid style mean that he never loses his readers in the labyrinth of his thought.

Starting from the premise of writing a book to explain why he is incapable of writing the book he wanted write, and which has been glimpsed in a dream (a permanently aborted project that would have involved poetry, mathematics and a novel entitled *The Great Fire of London*, which should have been, but clearly is not, the book in the reader's hands, hence the inverted commas that surround the title in the original French, and which have unfortunately been omitted from the translation) the result is staggering. Roubaud has not only led a surprisingly interesting life (a family home used as a base by the *Résistance* when he was a child; attempting to calculate wind directions during France's nuclear tests in the Sahara when doing his national service, to name but two examples from *The Loop*, the second volume), but he also has what has been called 'one of the literature's best furnished brains', his interests ranging from formal logic to poetry, via a number of languages including Provencal and Japanese, which he takes us through as lived experiences, with an expert hand, between the Scylla of obscurity and the Charybdis of oversimplification. Meanwhile, the overarching theme provides us with the finest mediation on time and its passing since Proust, to whose *A la recherche*, despite their obvious differences, this work has been justly compared, both for its scope and its achievement.

Felipe Alfau — Chromos [1990]

SAM MOSS

How do we address the persistent problem of one's identity? We are all simply and ineluctably human with little to suggest that we can be anything more or less. And yet we have this eternal drive to separate further, to dice ourselves in smaller and smaller groups, to separate ourselves from others and form in-groups and out-groups even to the point of absurdity. Even trickier, how do we ascribe identity to the immigrant, the exiled (willingly or otherwise), the traveler and the nomad? These groups not only lose their indigenous identity, but—in the end—are never *truly* able to gain their desired second identity (this is, almost always, the duty of their children or grandchildren) and end up somewhere in between with this third strange and misty identity. An identity which arises from the two-dimensional plain of (in Alfau's case) *Americanness* and *Spanishness* and forms a whole other axis, a whole other dimension to traverse, a space populated by such bizarre, multi-identified creatures as the Moor, Pedro Guzman the Chink, and so on.

Within this volumed spectrum lie two invincible points, two far off ideals forming a superimposed field on which every character (arguably every person, ever) must lie:

The spectrum of death.

It is incredible and pervasive, the degree to which death can bequeath or provoke identity.

At one end we have the American death: the finality of a joyous life lived in struggle against fellow men, a short struggle which inevitably ends in sorrow and pain, weeping and gnashing of teeth. This stands in stark contrast to the Spanish death, an event which occurs at some point in the already sorrow-filled life lived against nature (look at the bullfight, the epitome of Castizo culture, the man pitting himself against nature personified, a true minotaur at the center of the maze of life). The Spanish death is no end, no reason for sorrow, rather it is a shift to eternal glory, an ascension to ideal beauty. An inevitable move from the fallible to the infallible, the mundane to the holy. Think of the petrified notario or the senile man child Ramos whose deaths are not so much mourned as immortalized. To a Spaniard in Alfau's world death is the ultimate goal: fetishized by those homeland heroes such as the bullfighters, the pelota players, and the flamencos.

Alfau has himself stood between these two worlds and placed his sorry characters there in an exaggerated form. This navigation between identities, this navigation between deaths and the ultimate transcendence of both is the central question of *Chromos*.

Alfau gives us no answer, gives us no out. His postmodern sensibilities, unfortunately, make this an impossibility, which might be a good thing, however, since any answer to this tricky question, any solution to the problem of identity, would surely leave us in one place.

The grave.

Robert Alan Jamieson — A Day at the Office [1991]

RODGE GLASS

Before *A Day at the Office*, I wasn't awake.
I try and trace myself as I was in those weeks before I read what was, even then, a forgotten book. (It was published in 1991. I started University in Glasgow in 1997.) Was my hair long or short when I was a student? I couldn't cook, so what did I eat? Did I ever think about anyone but myself? And I can't answer those questions, not honestly anyway. Time has taken them to a place I can't access. All that's left is the story I tell when people ask me how I became a writer.

I do remember some things though. The smell in the hallway of my East End flat that I now realise was damp (but didn't recognise then); I remember the flash of sparks erupting from the extension cable when it gave out, the day I almost burned the place down and my flatmates said I couldn't be trusted with anything worth having; and I remember other things too, some of which feel, even now, like scenes from the *A Day at the Office*. Especially I remember the time my friend came to visit, his first time in Scotland, and nearly got our heads kicked in by the lads on bikes on the corner. (One of them dropped a packet of crisps on the ground as we walked by, trying to keep our heads down. My friend couldn't help himself. He went back, picked it up, and put the rubbish in the bin. I thought we were going to die.) These are all things I think of whenever *A Day at the Office* comes into my mind. I also think: we were lucky to get out. He's a Rabbi now. I'm fine. Neither of us are in the gutter Jamieson describes with such clarity and sympathy.

So this is a book that has lived with me since I woke up. But sometimes I wonder if I imagined it, as I've never met anyone else who's actually read it. In the seventeen years since I picked it up for the first time, only twice has *A Day at the Office* been mentioned to me by others —and on both occasions it's been by editors asking me to write something about it. After this time, I fully expect to not hear of it again for another decade when, hopefully, some other editor will ask me to source my battered old copy and contribute to keeping the book alive ... only just, maybe only for a few readers, but nonetheless, *alive*. It is, after all, a 'forgotten classic' so truly forgotten that almost no one has heard of it, and certainly only a few people could write about it. And yet, it had all the bravery and sense of entitlement of *Trainspotting*, two years before that book was published. It was liberating to read. When I was lying on the bed of my damp flat, extension cable smoking, no idea what I was going to do with my life, it presented to me poverty, hopelessness and fear in a way that made me feel like someone was reaching around my heart and slowly applying pressure, squeezing, squeezing. *A Day at the Office* made me want to avoid the trap being described in its pages. After all, back then I didn't know if I was going to end up turning into one of the characters.

Alasdair Gray — Poor Things [1992]

RODGE GLASS

A PERSONAL TAKE

Six years before *Poor Things*, Alasdair Gray wrote a little-seen, little-heard of pamphlet for the Saltire Society's Self-Portraits series. 'Meanwhile, what am I for?' he wrote. 'What does this ordinary-looking, eccentric-sounding, obviously past-his-best person exist to do apart from eat, drink, publicize himself, get fatter, older and die?' He admitted, 'At present I do not know.'

Though he published a great deal in the years immediately following this statement, Gray was mostly right. He produced 'novels' that had been plays decades before. He wrote political pamphlets that regurgitated previous ones. He wrote poetry about being dried up. But then, amongst all that, there's big, beautiful *Poor Things*. For a biographer, it's hard to explain, given the context. Not a repeat, not compromised, not taken on for much-needed cash. *Poor Things* won the Whitbread Novel Award, the Guardian Fiction Prize and even gave Gray readers in England. More importantly, it stands today as one of the author's greatest works. It's certainly his most playful, it unites word and picture beautifully, with humour—and that spills over into margins too. Some editions included fake erratum slips, fake batterings from the press, fake editors, all wrapped up in what's presented to readers as the 'daringly experimental history of Scottish medicine'. (This book is essentially a Glaswegian Victorian *Frankenstein*.) In short, *Poor Things* reads like a writer having fun. The opposite of the self-critical, exhausted, idea-less middle-aged man waiting to die.

And that's because he had someone who helped him forget he was now a public figure. Though Gray certainly felt under pressure in this period (in 1990 he published 'my worst book', *Something Leather*, cobbled together via rejected story fragments purely to satisfy a contract), his engagement as a writer wasn't purely about the world of publication, reviewers, events, interviews. (All of which he found draining.) Sometimes, he felt free, and with freedom, his imagination was unleashed in a way impossible when he felt watched. *Poor Things* was born because Gray was having weekly games of chess with his friend Bernard MacLaverty, the acclaimed author of *Cal*. At the time, Gray was writing a collection (later *Ten Tales Tall and True*) and read out parts of his works-in-progress to his friend between games. MacLaverty responded enthusiastically to an early version of *Poor Things*, originally intended as a story for that collection—and goaded him to keep going, go further, be more outrageous. Each time Gray brought back another five pages or so to read out, and another, and another, impersonating the voices of characters—until one day he noticed that much of a novel had been written. (Meanwhile, the collection he'd been working on was postponed.) For Gray, it has always been thus: the approval and encouragement of peers is a more powerful creative force than any other. It's no exaggeration to say that without MacLaverty, there would be no *Poor Things*. Which is why Gray did a (greatly distorted) portrait of him for the book's jacket.

W.G. Sebald — The Emigrants [1992]

PETER BEBERGAL

There is a famous question regarding a Jewish prayer that begins, "My God and the God of my fathers." Why do we pray to both "my God" and "the God of my fathers?" One answer explains that if we go to God only as an individual without tradition our faith is without structure, easily toppled. If we go to God only with tradition, then our faith is without heart and passion. So we must go to God with both. But what if the God of our fathers is absent? What if the faith of our fathers is a faith in secularism, modernity, and progress? What happens to the individual's faith when the God of my fathers doesn't exist?

A torn postcard is one of the only things left from my family's life in Poland. Written in Yiddish, it was a note from my grandfather Sam to his family in Poland while he was in Bremen, Germany just before he boarded the ship to America. On the other side is a photograph of the passengers of the ship. Some of the people in the picture are happy, something for them is about to change in a way none of them realize, but expectation is over all of their stiff clothes and bright eyes. Sam was to meet his father, already in America. Abraham Bebergal had arrived in South Carolina in 1899. "Father Abraham," as he was called by the African Americans in and around Charlestown, made a modest living selling various merchandise by horse and wagon to the poor black community. He eventually opened a department store in Charlestown, but still catered to the lower working-class blacks. He first sent for his oldest, who came to America by way of Ellis Island on the SS Freidrich Willheim. According to the ship's manifest, my grandfather Samuel, listed as Schlome, arrived on Ellis Island on August 25, 1913, final destination

Charleston, S.C. He is listed as being 5'1", red hair and blue eyes, from Zacrocym, 17 years old. It seems as though everything begins with that boy—Samuel—who sailed alone (amongst hundreds of other Eastern European immigrants) to meet his father already in America. Samuel was actually 14 years old when he was on the ship in 1913, coming to America from Poland by route of Bremen, and the wind is at his face and the salt of the sea on his tongue for the very first time.

What was Judaism for my grandfather as he left Poland? He was as close to it as one can imagine: Eastern European orthodoxy, a folk observance of ritual, tradition, all mixed with a heavy dose of superstition. When did he abandon it? On the slow train from Warsaw to Bremen? On the even slower ship from Bremen to Maryland? Was he giving up teffilin *and* God? Which one (or was it both) did he imagine incompatible with the life he wanted for himself and his family in America? And what did he leave me, what did I inherit, but an ache and some questions.

[Bremen, 1913. Waiting to board the Prinz Friedrich Wilhelm to Ellis Island.]

William Gaddis — A Frolic of His Own [1994]

CHRISTOPHER WUNDERLEE

William Gaddis matters ... He matters despite the lack of an obvious cadre of mimics reproducing versions of his work dangling from bookshop shelves. You cannot say who he has influenced definitely because he is that rare author whose laurels fit no one else.

He is an exception ... His exception is rooted in his facility for dialogue as a narrative instrument. In his books, *JR*, *Carpenter's Gothic* and culminating in *A Frolic of His Own*, it is the language of the characters that frames and coerces the essential elements of the story.

If the theatre is an illusion we accept, Gaddis twisted this conceit for another great illusion. You cannot ignore the genius of contorting one medium to advance that of another. And this exploit could not have been executed by anyone who without Gaddis' gift for the sound of varying voices.

"Language confronted by language turning language itself into theory till it's not about what it's about it's only about itself turned into a mere plaything."

A Frolic of His Own is Gaddis' great plaything; his language confronted by language turning language itself into theory till it's not about what it's about it's only about itself ... And this novel is all about itself. *Frolic* is that novel so believably satirical the reader accepts the absurdity of a man suing himself for running himself over with his own car after trying to break into it; of this same man suing a major motion picture studio for an unmade movie he ardently believes is based on his unpublished, unread play.

It is the pursuit of justice, and justice is supposed to be about validity, legitimacy, fairness, the truth; but justice is the synthesis of the law and "what do you think the law is, that's all it is, language". Anyone versed in legalese sees the satire.

Frolic is his ode to this linguistic paradox—the novel is filthy with lawsuits focused on defining expression as it relates to vaulted ideals—a sculptor v. a dying dog for instance—via dense legal opinions with all of its detail and strange combinations. Or excerpts from a play about a man who hires two soldiers to replace him during the Civil War for both the North & South who later kill each other in battle.

The central figures (Oscar, Christina, Lily, Harry) become known by their distinct voices—both how they define themselves and how others define them. We arrive at a full understanding of them only through their interactions. With everyone suing someone or some institution, arguing, making their case, defending themselves or another, justifying their actions or the actions of another, amidst a deteriorating family estate where the ailing Oscar wallows in legal chaos and crushing debt fantasizing about vindication and justice the full weight of their words accurately, paradoxically captures a unique realism.

Their interpretation is the interpretation turning interpretation into fiction, and so, it's not about what it's about it's only about itself turned into a grand experiment. And that's really why Gaddis matters.

Jáchym Topol — City Sister Silver [1994]

ALEX ZUCKER

"Mordy tvoyay keerpicha hochetsia! somebody screamed . . ." — *City Sister Silver*, p. 370

In 1994, Jáchym Topol's debut novel, *Sestra*, melted readers' brains like an electromagnetic pulse. Its impact on Czech literature was instantaneous, far-reaching, disrupting, and though nobody questioned its legality, like a weapon of mass destruction it provoked fierce debate about its effectiveness, usefulness, and morality.

Five years after communism collapsed in Eastern Europe, five years down the unmarked serpentine path "back to Europe", as they said in those days, Topol, up to then a writer of verse, rock lyrics, and reportage, unleashed a quarter-million-word torrent, a generational testimony attempting to render in language the breakneck, free-for-all change of "years 1, 2, 3, etc. after the explosion of time". Holed up in the German countryside in summer 1993 on a residency supported by the Heinrich Böll Foundation (depicted in the novel with sidesplitting embellishment), the then-31-year-old feverdreamed a version of reality so phantasmagorical some Czech critics were left wondering what had come from his head and what had actually happened: Was this their country? Did people really *do* these things? Sex, drugs, rock 'n' roll, OK; but human trafficking, snuff films? Magic charms? Silver bullets? People living in dumps? They hadn't read about *that* before. Not in a Czech novel.

Critics reviewing the English translation, *City Sister Silver*, for the most part threw up their hands, acknowledging the grand scale and ambition of Topol's project but dwelling on the centrifugal plot and the density and unfamiliarity of the references rather than digging a little harder to find interpretive handholds. At the same time, bafflingly, they tiptoed around Chapter 6, "I Had a Dream", a nightmare set in Auschwitz: central to the novel, featuring all its most important themes, and, one would think, an accessible entry point to U.S. critics. A saving exception among the Yanks was the late John Leonard, who in his review for *Newsday* ("I am sneaking sideways into a labyrinth") engaged *City Sister Silver* on its own terms.

What were those terms?

Homer, Dante, Dostoevsky, "Bowdlair", Anthony Burgess, Pynchon, Hašek, Čapek, "Rimbow", Graham Greene, the Strugatskys, Blake, the Brothers Grimm, Bulgakov, Babel, Karl May, MLK, and yes of course Kafka ... literature ... and language. Language is at the heart of Topol's novel, which may seem obvious—or should be—but for readers of translation, bizarrely, this is often forgotten. Our insatiable striving for community—a tribe to identify with, where we feel at home, accepted, understood—is for Topol bound up in language. Remember he grew up in the unnaturally, paranoiacally closed world of dissidents and the underground. Language, as it is in every subculture, was a fundamental way of setting themselves apart from the mainstream, in their case the conformist, materialistic, authoritarian society of the Czechoslovak Socialist Republic (ČSSR) in the years after the 1968 Soviet-led invasion to clamp down on the country's attempts to pursue a more democratic, less centralized path to socialism ("socialism with a human face"). The name the hardline Czechoslovak Communist leaders gave to this period —"normalization"—speaks volumes.

Viewed in this light, Topol's first novel was the continuation of a very personal, intimate struggle against normalization—and a first act of resistance against the new normal that began to take root with the introduction of market reforms and privatization after 1989. As Topol himself put it, while writing both *Sestra* and his second novel, *Anděl* (1995; Angel Station), "I felt like I was spitting in people's faces." In fact the "secret and open tongue of the Kanak kingdom" spoken by characters in Chapter 13 of *Sestra / City Sister Silver* can also be read as the language of the novel itself. "I'll write the book in raw post-Babylonian," Potok the narrator-cum-Topol alter ego declares, "the way I heard it on my wanderings through the past, present, and future." This affinity for rawness, equated with authenticity, was a hallmark of the underground culture that Topol grew up in, and still identifies with to this day. Elegance and eloquence as obstacles to communication; immediacy a priority. Because for all its branching and hyperbole, the novel—Topol—is always striving, desperately, to reach out to the reader. Reach your hand out to him and you'll find he's willing to meet you halfway.

Martin Amis — The Information [1995]

ANTHONY VACCA

*U*ntitled has a humble enough premise: "[W]ith its octuplet time scheme and its rotating crew of sixteen unreliable narrators, sounded like a departure [from his critically acknowledged but mostly unread, previous two books], but it wasn't. As before, all you heard was voice. This was the basket that contained all the eggs."

The Information's narrator presents Untitled as a hopeless endeavor, existing more as an escape for Richard from his disappointing life rather than an actual work of literary art for readers to admire. We are informed early on about Richard that "[a]lthough his prose was talented, he wasn't trying to write talent novels. He was trying to write genius novels, like Joyce." But don't mistake this as a stance of artistic aesthetics. Really, it's just because "Richard was too proud and too lazy and —in a way—too clever and too nuts to write talent novels. The thought of getting a character out of the house and across town to somewhere else made him go vague with exhaustion".

Richard's refusal of both a semblance of narrative and of any consideration for the reader can be seen cultivating within his previous two critically acknowledged—yet mostly unread—novels. "*Afterthought* was first person, *Dreams Don't Mean Anything* strictly localized third; both nameless, the I and he were author surrogates and the novels comprised their more or less uninterrupted and indistinguishable *monologues interiors*."

A turn of plot manages to bring Untitled (Oh, the hopelessness of that title alone!) into print, resulting in not merely just an incoherent bore, but an actual agent of malignancy. One reviewer "having spent fifteen minutes with Untitled on his lap, was admitted the same day to St.

Bartholomew's Hospital with a case of viscometer rhinitis. At present, he was in between sinus operations." It doesn't get much more metafictional than that!

Hell, even its appearance produces pain. "It was certainly a pity about the look of it, the look and feel of *Untitled*. No dust jacket, for instance; and that horsehair texture. Wrenching his first copy out of its Jiffy Bag, back in Calchalk Street, Richard had caught a hangnail deep in its bristling weft. And his fingertip was little more than a blob of plasma."

But what reader can't help but feel a perverse need-to-know when presented with the following: "The miraculously sustained tour de force in which five unreliable narrators converse on crossed mobile-phone lines while stuck in the same revolving door?"

I can't say that Martin Amis's *The Information* was my first taste of metafiction, but it certainly was the first lick of that particular literary device that had this reader writhing in linguistic ecstasy. But *Untitled* is such a small smack of pleasure within the verbal feast that awaits the lucky reader on every page of *The Information*.

William H. Gass — The Tunnel [1995]

H.L. HIX

A DISCOMFORTING TIRADE

At one point in his ravings, William Kohler, the awfully-similar-to-William Gass speaker in The Tunnel, declares, "Now I know how it feels to be lodged in a throat" (297). The Tunnel is not so much Kohler's tale as it is his persistent cough. He can't get rid of his phlegm. Kohler, it turns out, is boring, in at least two senses of that word: he is digging a hole in his basement, boring (as a beetle bores, or a worm) out of his home (such as it is) and out of his life (such as it is), and he is unexciting, able to conceive of himself only in terms tinted by the lens of world-historical evil and able to conceive of world-historical evil only in parallel to his petulance and pettiness. Pettiness*es*: he has plenty.

In an essay once, Gass declared that the "normal shape of a narrative (like an hourglass, it is so corseted by Time) and its customary content (its agents, actions, and their accomplishments) are both designed to disclose a comforting pattern in events, discover a true direction to existence, and give an honest meaning to life." If that's true, then The Tunnel is not normal, nor is its content customary. Kohler is digging a tunnel because his professing history—shaping and giving content to narratives—has *not* disclosed to him a comforting pattern in events, has not discovered to him a true direction to existence, has not given an honest meaning to his life. Which leaves him no comforting pattern, true direction, or honest meaning to offer the reader.

As fluent speakers of English have gone to their graves, replaced by freshmen, the word "discomfiting" has disappeared, replaced by the illogism "discomforting." But maybe "discomforting" applies to The Tun-

nel: it is not a normal narrative, but a discomforting, distrue, dishonest one. In a manuscript synopsis, Gass describes it as structured into "twelve Philippics."

That the book's parts take the form of denunciatory speeches—and not, for instance, incidents or episodes—indicates that the narrator's frame of mind will serve as the axis of the book's ambitions; around that revolve the otherwise not always obviously allied units of the book. No compensatory reality rights Kohler's listing mind, which means no comforting pattern secures *The Tunnel* against all the worst -isms: nihilism, solipsism, and the rest. If Kohler can be that cracked, so might I be. *The Tunnel* does not offer Kohler as an example—there but for the grace of God bore I—but as an irrefutable and unassimilable. Kohler cannot delight or teach. He can only bore, creating in both senses of "bore" an absence rather than a presence. Kohler is not there, and will never get there.

Gilbert Sorrentino — Red the Fiend [1995]

JENNY OFFILL

BETTER DEAD THAN RED*

> My mother groan'd! my father wept.
> Into the dangerous world I leapt:
> Helpless, naked, piping loud:
> Like a fiend hid in a cloud.
> —William Blake

This snippet from "Infant Sorrow" serves as the epigraph to *Red the Fiend* and it is this dangerous world that Sorrentino so brilliantly evokes in this novel, the story of a boy whose daily humiliations at the hands of his grandmother slowly bleed all the goodness out of him. That this heavily worked territory—childhood as a kind of hell—sparkles with new menace is one of the many surprises of this novel. Sorrentino, a writer often demonized as "difficult", has in fact simplified the story of childhood here until it revolves around just two poles, terror and hope. It is this question of hope, of whether or not it is useful to have it, that lies at the center of this extraordinary book.

Red, who briefly appeared in *Steelwork*, is a young Irish-Catholic kid, growing up in the flattened-out possibilities of Depression-era New York. After his father leaves, Red and his mother move in with her parents, crowding into their small apartment. In her daily catalogue of grievances, his grandmother makes sure that Red never forgets the

---

* Adapted from *The San Francisco Review of Books*, March/April 1995

debt she is owed for taking them in. It is one he can never repay for it increases each moment he breathes, eats, or sleeps under her roof. The ways in which she extracts her payment for this debt form the axis of torture around which the boy's life revolves. But more than Grandma's actions, it is her relentless voice, equal parts bitterness and malice, that shapes Red's world and everything he sees. The way Sorrentino uses Grandma's voice in this novel is nothing short of amazing. Even when Red tells his own story, it is Grandma's voice we hear. The world outside their apartment is filled with "floozies", "niggers", "wops", "coolies" and "cheating Jews". Red himself is "black as sin," a degenerate good-for-nothing damned to hell. The effect of this barrage of hate is overwhelming. Red sees no escape from this terrible voice, and there is also no escape for the reader either. Sorrentino gives us no resting point, no distantly glimpsed redemption. In simple, elegant language, he has built a place of no exit.

Grandma's perverse genius for ferreting out Red's fears, for thwarting his every desire recalls an old story about a man trying to build a foolproof rat-trap. The man asks himself, if I were a rat, is there anything in which I would have such complete confidence that to suspect it would be to suspect everything in the world around me?

The answer he comes us with is that the trap should resemble a common drain pipe, open at both ends, but with a trick spring in the middle. To suspect a common drainpipe, he reasons, would be to cease to be a rat. It is this sort of world in which Red lives, where every word, every gesture, every moment of respite is suspect, and the commonplace shines with menace. He is beaten for coming home early or coming home late, for wanting to stay in or wanting to go out. Slowly, Red realizes that whatever direction he chooses to move in will always be the wrong one. Soon he learns not to move, not to want or wish for anything.

Yet within this desolate landscape of thwarted desire and hope, there are a few tantalizing glimpses of what came before, of how Red and his family arrived at this place. Sorrentino is a master of list making and here he uses it to remarkable effect. One chapter begins "Red might be able to understand Grandma if he ever discovers who she has been obstructed by" followed by a list of her "obstructions" including everything from a "tawdry" Christmas tree to five pairs of beautiful shoes, never worn. Similar lists follow for Red's father and mother though here the operative words are *forgive* and *sympathize with* rather than *understand*. These lists are both remarkably funny and revealing; in one swift gesture, he pencils in the background for the horror story that is unfolding as Red is hammered into a monster. These chapters allow an unsettling moment of grace before the world shuts tightly around him again. It is a risky move for Sorrentino. Such explanations could easily have seemed sentimental or deflated the story's brutal power; instead they charge the novel with an almost unbearable sadness. Here is the cold, lost heart of Red's world, all the things he will never see.

One night, lying in bed, staring at the night sky, he "wonders why God who made these stars also made Grandma." The echoes here of Blake's *Songs of Experience* are, no doubt, intentional. Red in his way is asking the same question as the child in "The Tyger" who asks the fierce beast "did he who made the lamb make thee?" What little hope Red has managed to hide away depends on the answer to this question. For if he believes that the creator of the stars also created his tormentor, he is left with the fact that Grandma's malevolence is indeed the spirit of the world. His only other choice is to believe that nothing made the world, that its spirit is chaos. Here, Sorrentino subtly captures the moment when Red's world begins to unhinge itself from reason and design and become a remote thing, hurtling through space. The novel's ending is startling and perfect, an act of abrupt genius. I have read it many times but to this day it unnerves and inspires me.

Roberto Bolaño — *Nazi Literature in the Americas* [1996]

ADRIAN CARNEY

Nazi Literature in the Americas is at first an extended joke with an obscure punchline. The book, published in 1996 and translated into English in 2008, is an encyclopedia of fictional writers on the far-right, not just Nazis. This includes fellow-travelers, sympathizers, and other assorted cranks, nationalist soccer hooligans playing at political philosophy, eulogizers to weasels, and so on.

At first, it is not so apparent why Bolaño would spend so much time and effort to beat on such an easy target. He stitches together every mannequin of a writer before sending them to oblivion. I quote: "Halfway there she crashed into a gas station. The explosion was considerable." That's a mild example. But then the satire becomes more crude and vicious. Take the case of another writer who yearns for the ideals of sanctified marriage and a Christian theocracy like Francisco Franco's. She is married to a man who beats her. Now this is more than a joke, it's a person, sad and sympathetic.

Now you see the real purpose of *Nazi Literature in the Americas*. Though much of it is obviously unreal, it tampers with the understanding of what is real, and presents much of itself as though it were real. It creates an entire bibliography of artists who never were, but adds one or two real references to 'real' artists to ground the book in some plausible future. And now the Nazis mirror some beloved artists from our 'own' reality. Look, there's J.M.S. Hill, I mean Philip K. Dick. And here's Pedro Carrera, wait, Rimbaud. Here's someone who got in a fistfight with Allen Ginsburg. And here's someone who was trying to create a 'new Chilean reality'. But Bolaño was a Chilean. Wait, here's a Nazi board-game player who shows up in one of Bolaño's posthumous books. And here is the crucified Romanian general from the end of 2666. *Nazi Literature in the Americas* is intertextual, but even 'inter-real', as 2666 the book is real. Although by the year 2666 all of us will be no longer real, and only the wind will visit our graves and scatter the dust from our weathered tombs.

But this talk about graves and dust is the last part of *Nazi Literature in the Americas*, the chapter on the Infamous Ramírez Hoffman. The scales of the encyclopedia fall away, and the entry gives in to an extended personal anecdote. A journalist Bolaño (not our 'real' Bolaño) searches for Ramirez Hoffman, a writer who killed for Pinochet's dictatorship, and his art was in making bodies disappear, and in writing poetry in contrails. When Bolaño finds Hoffman, we see no creature of death, just a self-possessed man with melancholy eyes who warns Bolaño to take care of himself. There is no poet of death here. But in this search, we realize a fog-obscured reasoning behind of this project, his purpose for inventing this not-real literary tradition.

Geoff Dyer — Out of Sheer Rage [1997]

KATHLEEN HEIL

OUT OF SHEER LOVE*

*O*ut of Sheer Rage is about Dyer's "failure" to write an academic study of D.H. Lawrence, although he and we know that he never wanted to write a dry academic study of Lawrence in the first place. Dyer confronts the consequences the existential demand to choose his own adventure generate, as he is constantly obligated to define and question what it is that he desires while what he desires constantly changes and is redefined. He writes about the maddening ways in which we create our own problems and the even more maddening incapability we posses to adequately resolve them, whether the problem is not wanting to write, not knowing what one wants, or knowing what one wants but then changing one's mind because what one knows is left wanting.

To wit:

> "The important thing was to avoid awful paralyzing uncertainty and indecision. Anything was better than that. In practice, however, 'throwing myself wholeheartedly' into my study of Lawrence meant making notes, meant throwing myself *half*-heartedly into the Lawrence book. In any case, 'throwing myself wholeheartedly into my study of Lawrence'—another phrase which became drained of meaning as it spun round my head—was actually impossible because, in addition to deciding whether or not I was going to write my study of

---
* A version of this essay, in slightly different form, originally appeared in *The Rumpus*.

Lawrence, I had to decide where I was going to write it—*if* I was going to write it."

What Dyer does, and does remarkably well, is document inertia, frustration, boredom, indecision, despair, and a host of other shitty, very human emotions which we are almost always too proud or scared to ever admit to feeling to other people, much less to ourselves. He lays them out on the page and, rather than seeming the way they usually feel inside our scattered synapses, which is pathetic, embarrassing, shameful, or terrifying, he makes them, well, funny. Really, hilariously funny. Dyer makes comedy of the various ways we torment ourselves with our doubts and failures big and small. If I were French I would probably try to argue that the heart of Dyer's comic touch is the very darkness we suffer in our saddest hours, but I am not, so I'll just say I'd much rather be laughing with Dyer than crying alone.

Out of Sheer Rage gets into the human condition at its hairiest, and Dyer is so forthright as to the way he goes about it it makes me want to press this book into the hand of everyone I know, which I have more or less tried to do, which is more or less trying what I am to do now. You could put off buying *Out of Sheer Rage* to put off reading it because the possibility of reading it is more satisfying then having the book start and thus, ultimately, end, but putting off reading Dyer is really a step toward reading Dyer, which is what you want to do, not because what he writes is "Real", but because what he writes is what we live.

Alasdair Brotchie & Harry Mathews (Eds.) — Oulipo Compendium [1998]

JASON GRAFF

KIN OF A LIVING GOD

The quick brown fox jumped over the lazy dog. It made the elder Zeke question whether just having his old basset hound bring him the paper violated some codex of his animal-rights-crazy son. Boxing in old Zeke always made his youngest not just excited but without really proving it, seem quite the friend to all animals. To his son, the fox and the dog jumping across the yard was the very picture of animal equanimity, their little muzzles exchanging sniffs not in aggression but to find out as much about each other as they could. In the barn, young Zeke watched them from a top a dozen bails of sorghum boxed up and ready for the very July quail hunt he so adamantly opposed.

Father and son mixed it up a bit more in the zany old days than they're prone to do now, when they seem to take care to give each other just enough space to question the other's views silently. Of course, one of the consequences of that was that old Zeke and young Zeke grew apart in a way that to laxer judges of filial temperance might've proven beyond repair. Every complex father son bond comes to a kind of zenith from which the relationship will quiver and go jug-shaped.

Crazy as it sounds, neither Zeke could quite bring himself to justify praying for the dog or wavering on the fox. They were just two more living kin of a god waxing beyond the haze of equally imperfect people. Matters such as these, kind of just went unquestioned by each; lost as they both were in the vexing fog of providence's own moral maze. After all, every hunter has his own qualms of proof against the varying jig of life and each tax zone has its wicked boundary. Old Zeke watched them jump some more before quitting back to the house, newly admiring the fox.

Young Zeke remained camped atop that very jumble of boxes for quite a while longer. His thoughts zigzagged verily not so much between the quicker of the fox or hound but out amongst the crops of juniper and sorghum. They hadn't zealously cultivated any quintessentially useful crops since a June bug had hexed their soil to almost a swamp. Zeke clambered down from atop the boxes queasily; fazed a bit as he knew the jig would soon be not just up but over. The farm eviscerated as it was by the exacting machinations of a team of quizzical bank examiners was just not likely to ever again be productive enough to survive. Young Zeke equated the land and all its animals, foxes included, as a jeroboam from which poured the sweetest memories of his juvenility.

Finally, the fox left the hound enervated, wrecked and lying there quietly beneath a pile of juniper seeds awaiting a zephyr to spread them. Young Zeke took another in a long line of covetous final looks at the quarrelet of ground that had exacted such a toll from his parents and their parents going back generations to when the land produced the finest marjoram in the county. Juniper, sorghum, marjoram none of it could do much for Zeke or his father now, no equation of crops then in existence, no matter how varied would delay the baleful future. Still, Young Zeke, perplexed as he was by how it had happened, was determined to keep his face brave and quell the vilest and most jarring of his cogitations. Maybe the bleak quagmire of a future that he was always visualizing for himself would not come to pass, perhaps life's journey had a more exciting destination in store. Pity, young Zeke could only agonize about that which he saw as permanent with a taste for the nostalgia of barely remembered days that was nearly unquenchable and exhausted any objectivity he might bring to the situation. Just as he made his way back inside their hovel of a home, the dog, no longer quite so lazy, leapt for the fox.

Dubravka Ugrešić — The Museum of Unconditional Surrender [1998]

JASMINA LUKIĆ

A master of titles, Dubravka Ugrešić borrows the engaging title of this novel from the name of a real museum that existed in East Berlin until 1994, when it perished together with many other things from that time: the Berlin wall, Yugoslavia, the Soviet Union, communism . . . *The Museum of Unconditional Surrender* speaks about all of this, and much more.

Set in Berlin in the early 1990s, the novel brings together many disconnected personal stories and narratives about people who are trying somehow to make sense of the changing world and their own disjoined lives. The narration is fragmentary, but the connecting thread is the voice of the narrator skillfully playing with an autobiographical mode that is evoked and denied at the same time, and the shadow of an angel of oblivion who discreetly moves in the background. Although the narration moves to the other spaces as well, like Croatia and the USA, Berlin remains its anchoring location. 'Berlin is a mutant city', we are continually told, and this mutancy is what makes it a possible site for so much and so many interlocked (hi)stories.

In Dubravka Ugrešić's reading, Berlin is the city of migrants and artists, of those who speak from the margins. Being herself an exile of a country still at war at the time she was writing the novel, Ugrešić situates the experience of displacement at the center of her narrative. But she is not a writer who laments over exile; she is not nostalgic, but bitter and sharp, as much as she is warm and understanding for those who have to experience it. Hard as it may be, exile is also a liberating experience for her, since it offers a new freedom to be observant and critical.

If Julia Kristeva is right in claiming that in our times the dissident is the new type of intellectual, then Dubravka Ugrešić is an exemplary case of one such intellectual, being a dissident in both the political and the artistic sense of the word. A strong opponent of the nationalist ideology that has ripped Yugoslavia apart, and self-exiled from the region, she has left the comfort zone of national Croatian literature to become a transnational writer, one of those who write 'outside the nation'. As well as being a writer, she is also a public intellectual who continues to position herself on the margins, believing in their artistic, but also their critical productivity. In the 1990s she was first and foremost a critic of militant nationalism; in the 2000s, she turns her sharp, witty and inquisitive gaze more towards issues of globalization, its paradoxes, and its injustices.

The Museum speaks to both of these themes in her writing. The novel is masterfully crafted; every word has a meaning that should not be missed. It has a characteristic style that brings together profound reflection, sharp observation and a unique sense of humor which makes Ugrešić's writing so unique. It is a book which clearly shows why Dubravka Ugrešić's is recognized as one of the most important contemporary European writers.

Percival Everett — Glyph [1999]

TOM CONOBOY

Ralph, a ten-month-old baby, has an IQ of 476. He reads, memorises and understands everything that is put before him, from technical manuals to Immanuel Kant and, although eschewing speech, he writes and communicates fluently. This is the conceit at the heart of Percival Everett's satirical novel, a technique which allows him to view human life as an outsider.

Ralph is kidnapped by a crazed academic, undergoes a bungled kidnap by another and is kidnapped again by shadowy government agencies, where he is put to work as a spy. His travails don't end there. He is rescued by a kindly guard, only to be effectively kidnapped again as the guard and his wife, desperate for a child of their own, flee to Mexico. There, he falls into the clutches of a paedophile priest, while, one by one, his previous kidnappers and his distraught mother converge for a grand climax. Crazy? Certainly, and extremely funny, too. Don't expect dry social realism from Percival Everett.

Rather, he is a supreme satirist. At his best—in *Erasure*, for example—his satire is transformative. It could be argued, however, that he has a tendency to take potshots at everything, and certainly, with *Glyph*, the usual array of targets is lined up for an Everettian kicking—racial stereotyping, the media, church, academia, government. In *Erasure*, the targets are fewer and assaults more sustained, and it is all the more powerful for that.

Nonetheless, *Glyph* is enormous fun. Everett wickedly lampoons academia, particularly Roland Barthes—"I'm French, you know"—and postmodernist, deconstructionist literary theory. Barthes is a lecherous, pretentious buffoon, and Ralph joyfully debunks his treasured theories. Referring to Barthes' structuralist analysis of *Sarrasine*, *S/Z* (which also features in *Erasure*), Ralph agrees that, in theory, he could read a novel backwards or pull text randomly from it and so produce new fragments of work. "But I do not," he says, "any more than than I might walk the middle part of my trip to the refrigerator first this time and last the next."

As with all the best satire, though, there is a message behind the humour. Everett makes characteristic observations on race, religion and the evils of secret government, but this time his real target is truth. Near the end, Ralph insists that he "offers no truth about the culture", but he is being too self-effacing. The novel has revolved around truth, around the ways that we interrelate and how we prevaricate, how we come to judgements not based on truth but on our own prejudices and fears and self-interests. Ralph also insists frequently that, evidence notwithstanding, he is no genius. How could I be, he seems to be saying, because:

> What genius, I guessed then and know now, allows is the start of a new race. Genius means finding a way back to the beginning where the truths are uncorrupted and honest and maybe even pure.

And there we have it, the Rousseauian paradox that only by attaining the purity of less civilised ages can we grow more civilised, an act that is, of course, impossible. Ralph, our outsider, despite his massive intellect, is still pure, still literally a babe-in-arms, and for all his knowingness he represents that uncorrupted honesty we all seek but can never find. There is, beneath the satire, a tenderness in the writing of Percival Everett. He has the wit of a satirist, but the heart of a romantic. And, as Ralph tells us at one point, a romantic is "fond of a good story".

Percival Everett gives a good story.

Ali Smith — Other Stories and Other Stories [1999]

M.J. NICHOLLS

THE WRITER'S WRITER AND OTHER WRITERS

The Writer's Writer is not be to confused with The Writers' Writer. The Writer's Writer is a writer read only by other writers, whereas The Writers' Writer is a writer who writes on behalf of other writers. These are not to be confused with the The Writers Writer, who writes only about writers, or The Writer Writer, who writes about only one writer, known as A. Writer. The four writers met up to discuss being writers, their writing, and other writers. The Writer's Writer complained his writing was read only by other writers, and The Writers' Writer complained his work was written for other writers and no one credited him as a writer. The Writers Writer said that those qualities are what made them respectively The Writer's Writer and The Writers' Writer, and if they were any different they would simply be known as The Writer and The Writer, like the other writers. The Writers Writer complained that too many people were writers nowadays, and it was impossible to write about all The Writers out there, while The Writer Writer complained that A. Writer was hard to write as a writer, since he only ever wrote about the one topic: riders. The Writer's Writer suggested The Writers Writer should write about writers who had written a richness of writings and not the writers who had written little, and that The Writer Writer should write a new character, I. Writer, who wrote about writers who only ever wrote about riders. At that point, The Written Writer entered the room along with The Writ Writer, who issued the writers with writs for plagiarising the writings of The Written

Writer. The Writer's Writer burst out laughing and explained that The Written Writer was a fictional writer and a writer can't plagiarise writing from a fictional writer—whoever wrote The Written Writer was entitled to sue, but not The Written Writer itself, who was merely a written construct. The Written Writer and The Writ Writer were then written out by The Writer of These Writers, who wrote the other writers out too before they realised they were really The Written Writers themselves.

Ignácio de Loyola Brandão — Anonymous Celebrity
[2002]

RICKI AKLON

HATE EVERYONE ESPECIALLY YOURSELF

I foresee a meteoric rise to the bestseller lists with the novel I am writing: *Clara Was a Female Pig*. In this novel I am writing Clara is born in a pigsty, raised in a trough, and weaned into life with a penchant for rolling in mud. She overcomes her porcine beginnings to earn a PhD in Medieval History, and succeeds in the normal and uninteresting real world, apart from the occasional oink or two at parties.

PITY THE SATIRISTS

Spare a thought in this revolting era for the satirist. To satirise the deluge of self-satirising effluent that passes for populist entertainment and the pathetic vanity of a self-deifying movie industry is no mean feat in an age comfortable in its metameta cage. To be weaned in a world that values success, usually financial, above the pursuit of contentment, and to strive in a brattish and spoiled society where politicians fuck over artists in favour of financial dominance and votes, bestows the satirist his bile and cements his bitterness. To merry heck with the leaders who close libraries, theatres and community centres in favour of opening more retail opportunities and call centres to slowly mind-melt the populace. Fuck these zoot-suited capitalist cockslingers with their pus-filled polyps for souls. Because the only respite from the failed system in this failed First World is through literature—not through the ideologues, rhetoricians or motivational yammerers, but through the wondrous drug of fiction.

BLOOPER JUNKIE

I live for the blooper reel. Fuck-ups are to me a thing of art. The fluffed line, the fatal skid, the flat note. The unedited spectacle of human beings failing to do single thing right is at the nub of pure artistic bliss.

SEXUAL DYSFUNCTION AS GENIUS SIGNIFIER

Aristotle, Plato, Michelangelo—not one of these geniuses romped in the sand with a lust-wracked wench. I have attempted sex twice, once in the back of a Smart BoConcept where I climaxed on the leather seat four minutes before her readiness, the other in a forest with a pixie-creature who placed a spell on my sac after which champagne not semen flowed from my pecker. Both times I had a creative block for nine months and wrote little of my cosmological comedy *Ian's Ions*. Nietzsche, Spinoza, Kant—not one of these cheer-filled chaps engaged in vertical grunting with a desirous dame. I maintain that sexual failure makes for more transcendent art. Continual engagement opens up the sleazier oubliettes wherein Philip Roth *et al* writhe on their Eros-drenched mattresses exchanging unpleasant textual fluids. All I have to offer, my darling, is my genius. I have no rampant sexual organs with which to sate your lustful ways, please accept this short story 'I am a Simple Man' as a superior love-token.

THE BRANDÃO BRAND

This fantastically inventive satire comes blazing from the mind of a Brazilian powerhouse. A fame-dream fantasy gone fatal, the novel is rife with hilarious, ponderous, filthy and sharp reflections on the curse of ordinariness in a vapid and callous age, and contains some absolutely marvellous exploding fonts.

Curtis White — Requiem [2002]

TREVOR DODGE

WHAT'S THE SOUP, COOKIE?

First in Palmyra and then in Nauvoo, there was some dude who pulled some shit and went to some jail and died some death. About 150 years later, the great-granddaughters of all the women who loved him got together and decided to start a business selling scented wax. There was one that smelled exactly how apple pie smells when it's been left in the oven too long. And there another that smelled how an evergreen smells after you cut it down and stuff it in your car so tight and so full you find pine needles afterwards for years.

And there was even a wax that smelled how John F. Kennedy smelled that morning in Dallas. The great-granddaughters, they test marketed all the names for their wax except for that one, the JFK one. What it smelled like was all the candles in all the churches in all the world all burning all at once. Which is really to say that what it really smelled like, was the last bottle rocket you lit on the 4th of July, or Derek Jeter's jock after his last game at Yankee Stadium, or David Hartman's hair the morning after he quit hosting *Good Morning America* with Joan Lunden.

Which is also really to say that nothing ever smells like what it's supposed to smell like. Take Irish Spring. That's about the best example I can think of. Things don't have to be made into wax, either, for this argument to hold up.

Look, a father is dead. A father who had at least one son. A father made dead by an assassin. Or at least that's what every son who's lost his father thinks when his father dies. My father, he didn't *die*. He was *assassinated.* What is *that* supposed to smell like? The broken glass of a jailhouse window? A spring in Ireland? Pomade? Texas humidity? The questions we have about death, they are ridiculous.

But our ceremonies and songs about death, they are not. Our ceremonies and songs are important. Important because we can endure them even though we feel our necks tighten with every word and our chests crack with every note. These things, they won't waft away if we simply hold our breath. In the end, if we *don't* fill a book with ridiculous questions after our fathers die, well, what does that say about us? And in the end of the end, those big knots in our throats, well, they gotta smell like *something.*

Lucy Ellmann — Dot in the Universe [2003]

ALI MILLAR

KILLING LUCY ELLMANN

My first meeting with Lucy Ellmann was postponed, due to the inconvenient death of my grandmother. She got up one morning expecting to go to the beach after lunch and eat ice-cream, but the excitement of a routine broken stopped her heart in its tracks. My grandmother's that is, not Lucy Ellmann's. Lucy survived, and I do not know if she likes ice-cream, or the beach.

Two summers later as the sun beat the pavement back to tar and turned the ice in my latte to water, I sat outside with Lucy Ellmann, trying to shield my baby son's bald, hatless head.

That day she was overshadowed, not by my grandmother, but by—in no particular order:
 — Todd McEwen
 — Stuart Kelly
 — Vladmir Putin.

And here it is I expose my lack in Barthian terms. Lucy Ellmann, as a woman—a being—lives, with all her googlable accoutrements, and I cannot seem to escape that point as I try to write around her work. To ape is impossible, as is descending into sycophantic fandom. Instead I avoid the act of writing, and of remembering, and this whole thing becomes an object lesson in prevarication.

She is a small woman. So much so she makes me look tall, when I am not. She is short, and at the end of one arm—I cannot remember which —another lack—a notebook is attached, and as I speak she writes rapidly in it and I want to see what she's doing, but I cannot and already she has again outfoxed me.

The thing is, when I was young, I didn't like woman writers. I wasn't so young really when I said that. I didn't like them, I didn't like their concerns, I didn't like their style, and I sure as hell didn't like their book covers. I was ignorant, of course. And what Lucy Ellmann did was begin to solve much of the trouble with women for me. She does not write like a woman. For that you can pelt me with stones. Nor does she write woman in white ink, she writes to be read, and she subverts, and is wicked and funny, and hugely intelligent, and human. And that's what matters in a writer—what species they are, because there are plenty of inhuman ones; of both genders. Her stature grows.

Reading Lucy Ellmann was my necessary point of rupture, where the after cannot be the same as before. That day, which now seems too distant when the first snow of the season fell this morning, was also another chasm. After talking, plotting and planning, with Lucy Ellmann, I drove home across the city swollen with tourists to feed the baby. I sat cradling him in my arms only to read a plane had been shot from the sky over Ukraine and suddenly not just the male/female binary, but all of them, seemed pointless, academic and indulgent. I was in a rabbit hole, again.

Dubravka Ugrešić— Thank You For Not Reading [2003]

ANA STANOJEVIC

She's not Paulo Coelho, Joan Collins, E.L. James, or any other best-selling author that the masses are reading today. She is only an ex-Yugoslav/Croatian/Eastern European writer whose identity has been "blurred" not only because of the Yugoslav wars in the 1990s and her immigration to the Netherlands, but also (and maybe more so) because she's one of the casualties of the disappearing line between true literature and trash.

So why am I writing about Dubravka Ugrešić? Though in her collection of essays from the title she, perhaps too bitterly, complains about the state of tasteless "literature" today and the lack of real readers, we're still here and I'm sure we are not few. I've known about Ms. Ugrešić for a while, I've been seeing her name every year at the International Book Fair in Belgrade and I read her novel *The Ministry of Pain* prior to discovering *Thank You for Not Reading*. She's a name here in Serbia, as well as the neighbouring countries, even if it's only a name for a handful of people, not the masses. Her essays really made an impression on me.

The author's main premise and criticism in this book is the commercialization of literature. She is bitter about the lowering of literary standards, the dumbing down of the reading public, and the moving of focus from important literary and life themes to issues of whether an author is attractive enough to be on the book cover and whether or not his or her book has enough sex and violence in it. That's the stuff that sells, and therefore, the only thing that matters.

Any reader and writer who take books seriously will find the stuff in Ms. Ugrešić's book scandalous. She strips naked the publishing industry, fashionable editors who don't read, fashionable authors who pose, academics who are selling out for a few minutes of fame on TV, professors who are losing credibility via social media networks in attempts to become buddies with their students . . . She spares no one, but she does it in a light tone, trying to camouflage her outrage with humor.

So, how to make it on the literary scene today? Obviously not by being well-read, original, tending to the craft of writing. Well-written, quality books don't see the light of day, or if they do, it's thanks to independent small publishers who can't really promote them, so these well-read, original, worthy authors never get a chance to become recognized.

The Western countries have made a great business out of books and writing, notices Ms. Ugrešić. Not only are they publishing books based on jackpot plots and the authors' good looks, they are also organizing workshops and producing bestselling books on how to write a bestselling book. In order to fit into the big, well-rehearsed and everything-but-innovative publishing industry of today, the author needs to lose all originality, conform to the rules of globalization (where everyone from any corner of the Earth writes the same), change essential parts of his or her work according to their editor's whims, and smile for the cover photo.

Though not optimistic, Ms. Ugrešić ends her book with a story where she manages to slip through a hopeful observation: "There will be books as long as there are stories that are convinced they *must* be told, and as long as there are readers (and writers are readers, too!) who, reading these stories, are convinced they *must* elaborate on them."

The publishing world today is driven mainly by profit. Words, stories and *real* writers are driven by passion and the need to record an aesthetic, literary, political, intimate or any powerful idea or sentiment. Let's see which driving force survives.

Roberto Bolaño — 2666 [2004]

ALEX COX

At seven times the size of a novel's median word count and with nine hundred dense pages, *2666* requires commitment. Constructed over five parts, the opener, *The Part About The Critics*, relates how three academics seek to heighten the reputation of a reclusive German novelist, Benno von Archimboldi, in the hope of winning him a Nobel prize. For lovers of Bolaño's prior *The Savage Detectives*, it's initially disappointing: the protagonists are pompous and unlikeable, the prose restrained, even unadventurous. However, when joined by a fourth, female academic and in an attempt to find Archimboldi they visit the fictional Mexican city of Santa Theresa an eerie cloud descends. Their dynamic shaken, violent metaphors sprinkle over seemingly banal objects and we are can only conclude that Santa Theresa is the fractured core of something evil, if yet undefined.

The *Part About Amalfitano* follows: the protagonist here is a literature professor who guided our quartet around Santa Theresa in *Critics*, but the city becomes the central character, beset by poverty and desecration as *maquiladora* operators exploit cheap labour to milk ravenous north American consumerism. We discover that dozens of women who work in such places are murdered, and on an unbelievable scale.

The Part About Fate sees an American journalist, Oscar Fate, visit Santa Theresa to cover a boxing match, but is persuaded by Amalfitano's daughter to write about these murders, and to interview the prime suspect Klaus Haas, a German who remains incarcerated despite the murders continuing. The sinister miasma shadows every page, from depictions of grainy snuff films, the ferocity of boxing, and the presence

187

of shiny black sedans on street corners, ominous and menacing.

With *The Part About The Crimes,* that menace, arguably redolent of a writer hesitant to engage with his subject's brutality, spills over and almost overwhelms, as dozens of victims are found, the brutality of their deaths reported with coolness and devoid of sensationalism. Bolaño recounts each woman's clothing, her wounds and her job. Their similarities, coupled with the impotence of investigators, led by detective Juan de Dios Martinez, portrays the helplessness of a society where the only priority is in keeping neo-liberalism satisfied. The passage that affected me most was when Martinez, after finding another mutilated woman, visits a bar full of fellow officers and listens as the Police chief tells an endless stream of misogynistic jokes, each emancipating a laugh louder than the one before. Martinez never participates but he doesn't disapprove either. These women aren't murder victims, but casualties of a war in which only one side carries weapons.

Finally, *The Part About Archimboldi* sees us leave the catacombs of Santa Theresa and follow Hans Reiter as he confronts World War Two as a young German soldier, before becoming the novelist Archimboldi and ultimately, goes to Santa Theresa. The chaos of earlier sections is superbly balanced by the symmetry of the finale.

As Bolaño wrote *2666* he knew his failing liver would soon see him dead. In a morbid sense, that must have been liberating. He never had to think about critics or readers and simply wrote himself the finest book he could. His rage at the real-life atrocities carried out in Ciudad Juárez, where forty women are murdered or disappear annually, is delivered with the precision of a sniper. If Bolaño were healthy, I doubt the book would have displayed such wildness, so *2666* is flawed. But who needs perfection, when you have might?

Meredith Brosnan — Mr. Dynamite [2004]

JARLETH L. PRENDERGAST

MORNING PRAYER YEAR 2000 (HOMAGE TO O'HARA)

wake up
wake up
the drums of NOW©
in the Church of NOW are pounding!!
You live in New York
you big dummy
and the market's climbing
(well it *was*...)
up up up
through the roof ma!
It's a perfect spring day
but tomorrow begins
an endless series of
LONG COLD winters
—a new ice age though—
and the day after that no ozone at all
so get UP
put on your diamond-studded Prada thong
grab some passing genitalia
and SPIN!!!!!!!!!!
the ghost of Frank O'Hara is down the block
getting his poet's cock pierced
and (you saw this coming)
SUCKED

for a GALA birthday party at the House of Pain!
("That fucking hurts, man.")
How designer drug you look today Manhattan
with St. Bridget's steeple blasting out of
Cindy Crawford's gash
and solemn anemic children slaving
20 hrs a day in sweat shops
right here on Broadway!!!!!!!
like it was 1900 instead of 2000
which of course it IS
especially if they don't fix that Y2K shit
("Do you think your Wu-Tang sword can defeat *me*?")
& meanwhile
at brunch
in the sickly chic Colonial Café
on the NEW (scrubbed and gleaming /
no human filth on view)
Bowery
all my neuroses flow fast
like superfluid helium back into
LaChapellistic technicolor© nitemares
the queer couple
murdered (?) in O'Hara's poem
have guns 'n' mace 'n'
ninja throwing stars 'n' cellfones now
so don't fuck with us
blonde
clueless
homo-hating
Aryan Youth!!!
All down the line
long island junior thugs
dressed in Tweeds catalog
eurotrash knockoff suits

chosen by their stupid vain
habitually cheated-on girlfriends
engage in bloody pitched battles with
Sikh taxidrivers outside the Bowery Bar
(I saw this with my own eyes)
Hey do you remember
when the best thing happening
was Bettie Serveert?
now it's someone else
someone you've never even heard of
who's 12 and bisexual and legally blind
& living in Paramus Neu Jor-see
and she just bought "Rid of Me"
but there's no way to know
how could I know
no time to stop or catch breath
NO HOLDING BACK THIS FLOOD!!!
NO HOLDING BACK!!
may y'all & I & I be swept
faster and faster and faster and faster
ever onward
ever upward
forever and ever
with no regrets
(to speak of)
"sail on sail on sailor"
into whatever mindboggling
Farout Wiiiild aAbomnible
&/or
dElicious bBBIgggggg
igggg FfutureSssssss
may
BE

David Mitchell — Cloud Atlas [2004]

STEPHEN MIRABITO

In David Mitchell's debut novel, an ethereal spirit entity called the "noncorpum" transmigrates the bodies of different characters so it can control them and read their minds. By doing so, he inhabits the souls of hundreds people of all genders, ages, and ethnicities. As such, the noncorpum plays the role of different humans and mimics their behavior so that no one is the wiser. The search for its true identity drives the noncorpum to inhabit other bodies and through doing so unlocks the secret of its own inception.

Isn't it apt that one of today's most talented self-conscious postmodernists provides his readers with the perfect metaphor for his fictioning in his debut novel?

It is! And in Mitchell's third effort, *Cloud Atlas*, he exploits his "noncorpum" talents to their full potential. Often described as a set of Russian Matryoshka dolls, Mitchell takes a page out of Italo Calvino's *If on a winters night a traveler* to create a unique and compelling structure for *Cloud Atlas*: it's comprised of six different novellas, each one seated inside the one proceeding it: the first (and last) novella is a Melvillian romp split down the middle (mid-sentence) and placed at the beginning and end of the book. The second is an epistolary novella which recalls Christopher Isherwood in 19th century Europe (also split midway but placed second and second-to-last). The third is a 1970s airport thriller full of plot twists and corporate intrigue *à la* Patricia Cornwell, James Patterson, *et al.* The fourth novella is a *One Flew over the Cuckoo's Nest*-type story of Timothy Cavendish, a hapless book publisher who gets tangled up with the mob and thrown into an old folks home. The fifth novella is a take on Philip K. Dick set a few hundred years in the future.

And the sixth and final story—the whole and complete pearl at the core of the book—steals from Russell Hoban's broken english in *Riddley Walker* to create a post-apocalyptic vision of the future. After submerging through the first halves of the first five and the sixth complete novella, you rise to the surface again, finishing the second half of each story.

Phew! This all-you-can-eat buffet of genre would seem crass and "look-ma-no-hands" if it weren't so much fun. And like his noncorpum, perhaps Mitchell doesn't have a voice of his own and so "nothing to say" (extra air quotes around that bit of critical pretension) but damn does he draw you into his intricate and multi-layered worlds, and leave you entertained and dazzled.

Each voice he creates is so authentic that, as Mitchell puts it, "in a blindfold test . . . prose from two of my books could not be identifiable as having been written by the same person."

In *Cloud Atlas*, he traces human history with this narrative chameleon. Through emulating these voices (ranging from the 1800s to the 2300s), Mitchell executes his ambition to "to write the world, underlined three times, three exclamation marks."

Although the ill-advised 2012 movie adaptation hasn't done much for Mitchell except to obscure the book's plot and simplify its message, the original 2004 novel still has much to offer the contemporary canon. Read it and read it again!

Steve Katz — Antonello's Lion [2005]

W.C. BAMBERGER

The aesthetic sense is appetitive, Samuel R. Delany has told us. That is, it doesn't rest listlessly in the bottom of our brain like an axolotl in a tank—rather for those of us with a taste for the forms an idea might take to move itself out of someone into the world where it can be gathered in again, this sense is as restless as a sawshark, constantly moving, seeking satisfaction. So it is that I have been through hundreds of authors, thousands of books, and after the silt settled I have found that Steve Katz has not only written more amazing and original fiction than anyone else I've read, but he also has exponentially expanded my idea of what fiction can do. For me, Katz is our most important living novelist.

I first encounter Katz's work by way of *The Exagggerations of Peter Prince*, from 1968. I've followed his pages through the metafictional gamesmanship of *Creamy and Delicious;* the absurd, quotidian and deliriously romantic *Saw*; the deadpan photo narrative and autobio journeying of *Moving Parts*; the daunting and encyclopedically style-inclusive *Stolen Stories* (for me, THE short story collection in English of the past fifty years); the great 1980s threesome of *Weir and Pouce, Florry of Washington Heights* and *Swanny's Ways*, and more. In *Antonello's Lion*, from 2005, Katz gathers himself to tackle one more time the question of what it is that people (and nations, and the world as a whole) think they are doing to and with one another. He does this brilliantly, with dazzlingly casual proletariat surrealism (rich people have a chip inserted at birth that allows them to float above the poorer population, for example) and the kind of open-heartedness that pierces our cynical American shell by its unabashedness and copper-penny-simple honesty.

In *Antonello's Lion* obsessions abound. The primary ones belong to Solomon and his son Nathan. In Venice in 1962, Solomon is driven out of the apartment he shares with his painter girlfriend by her egocentricity and heartlessness. Solomon goes off in search of a lost, perhaps even non-existent, painting by the Italian Renaissance painter Antonello da Messina and he disappears. In 2001 Solomon's son comes to Italy ostensibly for a vacation, but becomes obsessed with his father's fate, and goes off looking for him.

Beginning with this simple narrative armature Katz weaves a dizzying succession of events, often in parallels and variations, as if writing a fictional fugue. Solomon leaves his vain preening artist girlfriend (Nathan's mother-to-be) behind and she becomes a famous, if stagey, painter and indifferent mother to Nathan. Nathan escapes his nurturing, caring girlfriend and nearly disappears himself. In the end he makes his way back to an America under attack both from without and within, ultimately gathering to himself a small spark of hopefulness, and one person to share it with, leaving us with both the dispiriting idea that they may be the only two left not consumed by obsessive destructiveness—and the optimistic notion that two may well be enough. This novel will expand your sense of what fiction can do and warm your nights, as well.

Graham Rawle — Woman's World [2005]

MICHAEL LEONG

On the front of the dust jacket to my copy of Woman's World there are two blurbed quotes beneath the author's name. Joanna Lumley (of Absolutely Fabulous) says, "I think Graham Rawle may be a genius," a statement which is echoed and reinforced by the Times blurb directly below it: "This book is a work of genius." The distinction between "may be" and "is" aside—in what ways can we say that Woman's World is, indeed, a work of genius? In "Portraits and Repetition," Gertrude Stein famously described a "genius" as "one who is at the same time talking and listening" hence shifting away from a still popular notion of the work of genius as a transcendent monologue of original creativity towards a dialogic model of split attention involving both sending and receiving, articulating and understanding. I want to suggest that Woman's World is a work of genius in this somewhat idiosyncratic Steinian sense: that its intricate process of composition makes it (much like the book's unreliable narrator, who has a split personality) at least two things at once.

In an important process note at the end of the book, Rawle explains that he composed the 437-page tome that is Woman's World by collaging together approximately 40,000 textual fragments cut from women's magazines from the 1960s, magazines such as Woman, Woman's Own, and House Beautiful. This is to say that Rawle's engaging melodramatic thriller emerged from the re-constellated ruins of mass culture. Woman's World, then, is both text and image (or the image of text), representing a meticulous act of both reading and writing, cutting and pasting. Woman's World is also both a fictional narrative as well as a creative analysis, an immanent critique, of 1960s domestic culture and gender ideology. It is a tremendous feat of constrained writing (which took Rawle five years to complete) in the tradition of Oulipo (*Ouvroir de littérature potentielle*) but without the esoteric mathematics.

More importantly, the effect of reading Rawle's book, which is beautifully printed in facsimile so that we can enjoy its playful orchestration of various fonts and inserted illustrations, is that of encountering an epic ransom note "written" by a master designer-*cum*-compulsive collector (in a wonderfully self-reflexive moment Rawle's narrator says, "My dressing room is piled high with all the women's magazines I have saved over the years. Wouldn't it be wonderful to collect together my favorite fashion features, all the hints and tips on glamour and etiquette that I have found especially useful, and keep them together in one big book?"). The novel's visual element is crucial: just as, in cinematic melodrama, the sentimental music of the soundtrack indicates the emotional excess of the scene so too does Rawle's lively *mise-en-page* act as a kind of "graphic soundtrack" to the narrative. For example, in a moment of tension, when Roy's girlfriend Eve finds a strange brassiere in his van's glove compartment, the word "BRASSIERE" (no doubt a word derived from a magazine advertisement) conspicuously appears in the text in a large font highlighted by a dark background. There are many such moments in the book, which always remind us that what we are reading is, in fact, a product of numerous voices, voices to which Rawle has carefully attended.

Gilbert Adair — The Evadne Mount Trilogy [2006-2009]

MANNY RAYNER

WHO KILLED AGATHA CHRISTIE?

"Now," said Evadne Mount in her quiet but implacable way, "I shall ask you all to join me in the library."

"*All* of us?" asked Gilbert, sardonically lifting an eyebrow.

"That is what I said, Mr. Adair," replied the renowned amateur sleuth.

"But there is only me," said Gilbert.

"Only *I*," said Evadne with a hint of impatience. "And frankly, how many of you there are is hardly the question. I would like to observe the proprieties, even if you don't."

"But be reasonable!" entreated Gilbert. "How can we have a mystery with only one suspect?"

"I do not intend to continue this discussion," said Evadne, as she opened the door. "Please accompany me. Or would you rather that I detailed my sordid experiences with Cora when we used to share that little apartment? I recall that she was rather fond of licking my—"

"You can't say that!" yelped Gilbert. "It would be unthematic and out of character!"

"I am merely making a point," replied Evadne. "I no longer work for you and I will say what I like. Now shall we start?"

Defeated, Gilbert followed her.

*

"Very well," said Evadne, after they had taken their seats. "Let us review the facts. A murder has been committed here, a murder most foul. The standard Agatha Christie formula, one of the most beloved traditions in English literature, has been cold-bloodedly done to death."

"But—" interrupted Gilbert. Evadne ignored him. "Done to death," she continued. "By you, Mr. Adair, as you rightly say, the only suspect. The question is—*why?*"

"It was more an hommage—" began Gilbert, but again Evadne cut him off.

"Let us not waste our time. I think we can both recognize hommage when we see it. To call what you have done hommage insults your own intelligence as much as mine. You have subverted, Mr. Adair, you have used postmodern narrative techniques, you have"—her eyes narrowed to slits—"you have referred to Proust. We're talking premeditated murder here." She paused. Gilbert's shoulders slumped in dejection.

"Good," said Evadne after a moment. "And so, once again: why?" She waited in vain for a reply. "I considered various alternatives," she said. "Maybe it was just a joke that went wrong, a light-hearted parody slipping out of hand." Gilbert looked for a moment as though he wanted to say something, then thought better of it. Evadne smiled mirthlessly. "Quite so. A reasonable explanation, perhaps, for something shorter, less substantial. Here, we have nearly three hundred pages. Rather a lot, I think you'll agree, for a joke. What else?" She dragged on her cigarette and blew out a reflective jet of smoke.

"At several points, you unsubtly insinuate that Christie is racist, in particular antisemitic. Very clever. A defense that would surely win you the court's sympathy, except that it explains no more than a fraction of the novel. Once again, we come back to the same problem: why is there so much of it? What literary form requires such inordinate length? I kept turning the question over in my mind, and then the Labrador was shot. Do you remember what I said?"

Gilbert's face grew haggard, his bravado quite gone. "You said, 'Of course'", he replied in a barely audible voice.

"Indeed I did," said Evadne, pausing again before administering the final thrust. "Indeed I did. What was the point of the only narrative form which combines excessive, pointless verbiage with a childish pleasure in constructing *jeux de mots*? You, Mr. Adair, have written this book in order to create a shaggy dog story. What do you say?"

Gilbert stared at her with hate-filled eyes. "You'll never be able to prove it," he whispered.

Evadne shrugged. "That will be for the jury to decide," she said. "And now, Constable, I think it is time for you to take over."

Nicola Barker — *Darkmans* [2007]

KINGA BURGER

There are various volumes on the market called 'Life in the UK'. They are usually a laughable 200 pages long and preposterously claim to teach foreigners everything they need to know to successfully fit into British society. I pick them up and flip through them half-heartedly, thinking it's about time I applied to become a subject of Her Majesty but quickly I abandon them and instead I find myself going back to *Darkmans* by Nicola Barker, which to me explains the baffling experience of living in the UK more competently.

It all happens in the drab little town of Ashford, far from the cosmopolitan London, which no longer knows anything about being English. It's all here—the past and the present, chavs and NHS employees, construction workers, small-time criminals and immigrants—all haunted by the ghost of John Scogin, a wicked medieval jester, who muddles their minds and makes them speak in tongues (or something resembling pre-Shakespearean English to be precise). Half the time the characters don't know what (or who) possessed them and they bumble along trying to get on with their lives unaware of the bigger forces that rule them all.

The reader thrown into this grotesque narrative is as confused as any newly arrived immigrant. The impressive scope, the research, the linguistic finesse of *Darkmans* gives the impression that Barker is a very serious writer but it's possible she is just telling jokes with a straight face. It's something the English do and recognising such behaviour should be a topic covered in 'Life in the UK' booklets.

An immigrant who chooses to read *Darkmans* will also learn a valuable lesson on the neverending English battle with history. History haunts and hunts the English relentlessly. They wrestle with it, put up an admirable fight but ultimately always lose. Any newly naturalised citizen of the United Kingdom would do best to remember that from now on history will be their shadow everywhere they go, that won't leave their side even at night.

In this alien landscape Barker offers her foreign readers one point of reference. It's Gaffar, the Kurd immigrant who is allowed two registers —simple broken English on one hand and a highly eloquent ornamental Turkish on the other, but of course only one makes it through to his listeners. Let that be the final warning for all aspiring British citizens.

So forget 'Life in the UK', read *Darkmans* instead. Its 800 pages might not cover all of the UK but these do a way better job explaining at least 'Life in England' than any government issued leaflet could ever hope to do. It will make you break out in cold sweat every now and then, it will haunt your dreams and turn them into nightmare accompanied by a sinister cackle of a medieval jester but if you can survive this reading adventure, you're ready for this country where life imitates art.

Lydia Davis — Varieties of Disturbance [2007]

ALI MILLAR

THE RAT KING

Prologue

At three minutes to six the doctor is running late with five women left to see sitting on their choice of seven chairs outside his office. This doctor of woman is a man, and so carries the whole human race within him and therefore is already more than them; but nonetheless, cannot keep to time.

#1

'CLEARING SNOW KILLS' she reads, giving her the title for her next piece 'After Beuys or 57 Ways to Die', which will mirror last year's '57 Words for Mother', which, when she'd phoned her own she'd planned to call art, not life. But the phone rang out, in much the same way as it had last night.

#2

Worries, now unable to avoid, and if rendered a void—as she will be—how then to fill the hole. Funny what the removal of a letter does. If she no longer carries that which makes her woman, is she less than man, reduced to an? If simply a prefix, will she be useless, or used less?

Dream

In the dream she has lost her mother, hinting at a certain lack of care she does not possess in waking. She finds a mass of tangled tails with rat bodies wheeling out from the centre—variations in size implying varying points of decline. She'd scream if she could, for she very much wants her mother back.

#4

She sneaks a peek into her mirrored compact. Before leaving the house she'd made herself up, now the fiction threatens to slip. Her face is no longer a blank canvas but instead is lined and marred, reminding her of when, at the age of three, she'd asked why her mother's nose looked so much like a strawberry.

#5

Strange to be thinking now of potatoes, but rather that than this, of Grandpa pouring over his seed catalogue, circling the desired varietals red. Then in the autumn, when grown fat and distended, they'd eat them with beef or chicken or pig, and he'd talk about them being waxy or floury or disappointing. How she hates potatoes!

Epilogue

Behind the door sits the doctor with his head on his desk, moving it occasionally to find a cool spot.

He's had enough of women today.

He wishes for an ovary depressor or a hysterical label, for ignorance and dark ages.

When young he'd liked the words they used; malignant and metastasised, liked too the way saying them made him feel. Now though, overused they'd lost all meaning to him, but not the women he gave them to. They always managed to look surprised their insulating money and trim figures had not saved them. The fates never were choosy.

Later, they will drive him to drink, but first he must tell her the news.

Lydie Salvayre — Portrait of the Writer as a Domesticated Animal [2007]

JULIET JACQUES

I am the writer as domesticated animal in Lydie Salvayre's *Portrait*, with a few differences: I'm not French; I'm far younger, and when her novel was published, I had not started my transition from male to female, although I had by the time it appeared in English, in William Pedersen's translation; I haven't taken the specific, self-sabotaging step of agreeing to write the authorised biography of the world's richest man, expected to record his every opinion and enact his every desire.

But I am her, and she is me—introverted women, writers whose lack of confidence and fiscal independence lead to some awkward compromises, agonising over how much their masochistic fantasies have pushed them there. In return for the huge salary that she hopes will set her up for life, the author is told what to wear and how to comport herself (which reminds me of my negotiation with the Gender Identity Clinic, who controlled my access to hormones and surgery), alienating her literary friends, and there's an unescapable sense that any relationship between artist and funder is a game of dominance, submission and humiliation.

Tobold, who makes her tell visitors that she is his escort, is utterly repugnant, resembling not so much of real-life tycoons or literary businessmen so much as Monty Burns of *The Simpsons*. A libertarian monster who sees Christ as "the first worldwide advertising giant", and who wants the book to spread his evangelical belief in the Free Market, he endlessly pushes her intellectual and sexual boundaries, as the author is constantly disgusted at what she finds herself enjoying, and confused about whether she has consented.

This begins with the glamorous celebrity parties where she dances with Robert de Niro, reminding me of how I pursued mainstream journalism rather than the exploratory fiction closest to my heart, then was seduced by invitations to the House of Commons and other prestigious venues until I finally acknowledged that I found them more disgusting than fascinating. Like her, I associated failure with literary merit; like her, I voluntarily receded from these circles and felt ostracised in return, left only in dread of that existential question: *What do I really want?*

Like her, I've found the idea of not having to look after myself, or my finances, appealing after years of draining struggle, especially if I could abandon the 'militant asceticism' that I thought necessary to write. I'm aware that men like Tobold destroyed the infrastructures that might once have supported us, eliminating our options, forcing us to operate on their terms, ensuring our hypocrisy and drudgery. That's not enough: Tobold is determined to convince her that literature is useless, that only *business* matters; in that, he's like the sociopaths who decide Conservative economic and cultural policy. Unlike her with Tobold, I didn't nominate them as the people whose desires I *might* be prepared to fulfil, but their ideology has still got under my skin, and I have no hope that its foundations will be rocked in the way that Tobold's are, near the end of Salvayre's novel. Instead, I continuously find myself wondering where I'd stop in trying to dispel worries about money, and if I'd be turned on by prostrating myself before the people who most repulse me, remembering those despicable moments when I shook hands with MPs, and hating myself.

Adam Thirlwell — Miss Herbert [2007]

JACK ROSS

Dear Mr. Thirlwell,

Permit me to introduce myself.
I am, in and *of* myself, of little interest. My name will not mean much to you, still less the fact that I was (until retirement) a teacher of French language and literature.

Were I, however, to inform you that there has long been a tradition in my extended family that it was my Great-Great-Great-Great-Great-Aunt Juliet who was the "Miss Herbert" once privileged to instruct Gustave Flaubert's niece in the rudiments of English style (as well as— possibly—her uncle . . . in various other matters), you might perhaps be more readily inclined to listen to me.

The title of your fascinating book seized my attention immediately when I saw it in our small local bookshop (remaindered to clear, I'm very sorry to say). I was especially intrigued to read the passages on pp. 29-30 and 87-88 where you describe the relations between the two (albeit an account substantially indebted to Hermia Oliver's *Flaubert and an English Governess: The Quest for Julia Herbert* (1980), as you acknowledge on p.440).

You also quote, on p.29, from one of the Master's letters to his best friend Louis Bouilhet: "at table my eyes willingly follow the gentle slope of her breast. I believe she perceives this. For she blushes five or six times during the meal," following this with another quote praising the contours of "Miss Herbert's" bottom!

But I should get to the point. *Not*—alas—the discovery among family papers of her famous lost translation, completed under the Master's own eye, of *Madame Bovary*, but of a single scrap of paper, which may or may not be in her handwriting (no unequivocal samples of which have survived), in one of my Great-Grandfather's books, Ford Madox Ford's *Joseph Conrad: A Personal Remembrance* (1924), opposite the phrase: "the first words of Conrad's first book were pencilled on the flyleaves and margins of 'Madame Bovary'" (p.7), containing some scribbles which *do* appear to be an attempt on the very first sentence of that novel:

> Nous étions à l'étude, quand le Proviseur entra, suivi d'un nouveau *habillé en bourgeois et d'un garçon de classe qui portait un grand pupitre.*

This is Eleanor Marx-Aveling's 1886 translation:

> *We were in class when the head-master came in, followed by a "new fellow," not wearing the school uniform, and a school servant carrying a large desk.*

The scrap of which I have just spoken, however, reads:

> *The school bell had just struck half past one when the Head-master entered our classroom, followed by a "new bug" in mufti and a servant boy bearing a large desk.*

The word "mufti" surprised me most of all, I must say. However, my *Shorter Oxford Dicionary* does confirm this usage as dating back at least to 1816. The addition of a striking clock to Flaubert's opening phrase also gave me pause, though I note that this variant is recorded as belonging to the "*ms. autographe, dans son dernier état, après correction*" in the 1971 Garnier edition of *Madame Bovary*.

This might perhaps be taken as evidence that the translation in question was made from the "author's own manuscript" rather than any *printed* edition of the novel—which might, in turn, allow us to associate it with that fabled lost version.

Who can say? It may be a complete coincidence. Such as it is, I offer it to you in homage.

Urmuz — Complete Works [2007]

EDDIE WATKINS

Urmuz's world (henceforth Urmuzia) is a crowded world, invigorating in its genital and intellectual eroticism. Urmuzia is not only crowded with objects and people, but with ideas reborn as objects; idea-objects to be lived among as one lives among edible badgers and the shopkeeper's quivering beard. Urmuzia is so concentrated with meaning and significance, which in Urmuzia constitute a kind of eccentric intellectual gravity, binding and freeing, that space and time continually collapse into themselves, bending the reader's mind and rendering all events nearly simultaneous (unless viewed through an horological magnifier) and all space continuous and overlaid. This gravitational collapsing, or warping, also draws mythical beings (Venus and various Nymphs) into the dense urbanism of Urmuzia, making of Urmuzia an enchanted land packed with togetherness, metaphysical pursuits, fatalities, and beaks made of aromatic wood.

Urmuz's *Complete Works*, thirty-three pages long, is too expansive in its tininess, too completely a small infinity, to be covered in its entirety in this squib; so I will focus on his novel *The Funnel and Stamate*, which at five pages is the shortest Victorian-style family epic that shoots into extreme metaphysical pursuit in existence.

It opens in the compact and labyrinthine abode of Stamate, his wife, and their son Bufty. They live underground in a room connected to the outside world by a(n) (alimentary) canal. Above are two rooms accessed by a trapdoor—a sumptuous Turkish room, and a windowless room with the essence of "things in themselves" on a legless table (idea-object of pure being). In the windowless room is a communication tube through which all of space and time can be viewed, as well as dry biscuits and a residual matrix of cosmic determinism. Though tied together to a pole for most of the day the Stamates' life is roughly utopian. They live as children, gazing at Nirvana (just down the street next to the grocer's) and bombarding it with pellets of bread. For kicks they flood the windowless room and shoot off pistols. When an alien Eros enters the idyll . . . Just as Stamate touches pure metaphysical truth, the other side of "things in themselves", Nymphs distract him into lusting after their funnel. He plants the funnel beside the communication tube (marrying the mind and the genitals), and a new golden age for Stamate begins. Until Bufty humps the funnel . . . Stamate tosses Bufty and his funnel-lover into Nirvana (where, paternally, he sets up his son as a clerk); then hugs his wife and sews her into a waterproof bag (affection pervades Urmuzia, even as eccentricities often isolate individuals, making relationships barbed and even violent). Stamate then shrinks himself and runs to penetrate and disappear into the small infinite. He is still running.

Running deeper into Urmuzia . . . Urmuzia is embodied Einsteinian space-time, with Kafka's ears and eyes, pedalling Jarry's bicycle (and packing Jarry's pistol), while playing Einstein's violin through a demented Dickensian bohemia; where everything, even pure ideation, is tangible and erotic, and where Urmuzians strive to vanish back into the intangible.

Marilyn Chin — *Revenge of the Mooncake Vixen* [2009]

MELANIE HO

ON FOOD

Sometimes I think that if it weren't for food, I wouldn't know my grandparents at all. When we used to make summer pilgrimages from suburban Ottawa to my mother's hometown of Vancouver, food was just about the only thing planned in advance. My mother could eat everything she missed; for my sisters and me it meant far more Chinese food than we were used to and a chance to eat my grandfather's pancakes and peach pie. His pie crust recipe used vegetable shortening and is probably outdated, but it remains the one I use today for apple pie at Thanksgiving and tourtière at Christmas. I wouldn't switch to a butter crust—at least not now.

With my grandmother, food has always and continues to substitute conversation. I couldn't tell you her birthday or talk about how she felt working three jobs after immigrating in the 1960s, but every time I see her I know to take her for fish and chips. I'm not even sure why she likes it—it could be from working at a salmon canning factory, or maybe simply because Vancouver is by the water and she likes fried food.

It's through these wordless connections that I think I understand what it means to have Chinese heritage (beyond the obvious black hair, almond-shaped eyes, and yellowish skin) and at the same time to have grown up Canadian. When visiting my grandparents we sometimes used to eat stuffed glutinous rice dumplings called *júng*. I think they taste awful, but that's not really the point. After unwrapping the dumplings from their lotus leaves, we used to soak the rice in maple syrup to make them palatable. It was only when I moved to Hong Kong that I realized that maple syrup isn't their natural condiment.

If someone were to ask my biggest regret of not speaking Chinese, it would have nothing to do with job prospects or getting ripped off at the market, but the fact that outside of food I don't know my grandparents. We've never spoken the same language. My mother has always acted as an interpreter between my grandparents' Cantonese and my English with its earnest *jou sahns* pronounced in totally the wrong tones. I will never have stories about my grandfather's time as a pastry chef on an Alaskan cruise ship or about the life he left behind in Hong Kong, but I do have memories of eating ice-cream together and using coffee mugs to measure out flour for pancakes.

This is neither a confession nor a celebration (it's also not a proclamation that food *is* language). But perhaps through food I can build years and decades and, hopefully, generations of memories, memories that don't require anyone to say anything. After all, with baking, it's all in the hands.

Where words have proven inadequate, I have instead a wok-wielding grandmother and memories of a grandfather with his pastries baked from memory. That and a kitchen that smells pretty good.

Gabriel Josipovici — Only Joking [2010]

GIANNI DANE

Barbara Wright rightly writes in her 1958 preface to her 99 exercises à la mode Queneau that:

> Queneau... doesn't take himself over-seriously. He's too wise. He doesn't limit himself to being either serious or frivolous... a scientist or an artist. He's both... the reason why you find people in England who don't know who Queneau is. Two of his novels were published... not very successful[ly] here... the critics thought they were writing favourably about them... Queneau's wit and lightness of touch [is] possibly misleading—the book's very brilliance seemed to blind the critics to the fact that it was about anything... it seems that if we are to enjoy anything then we must not have to think about it, and conversely, if we are to think about anything, then we mustn't enjoy it. This is a calamitous and idiotic division of functions.

A small piece of history surrounding the publication of Josipovici's *Only Joking* explains the relevance of that quote. The book was first released in Germany as *Nur ein Scherz* in 2005 (translated to the German by Josipovici's friend Gerd Haffmanns), and published by CB Editions *after* Josipovici, writer-critic, Professor Emeritus at the University of Sussex, and reviewer of Christine Brooke-Rose's fictionalised autobiography *Remake*, had been misquoted from his book *What Ever Happened to Modern-*

ism? to great fanfare in The Guardian* in 2010. Josipovici replied in September of the same year, in The New Statesman:

> One of the minor themes of my latest book, Whatever Happened to Modernism?, is that a grave problem with cultural life in Britain today is how all issues are reduced to a question of personalities. I learned just how true this is when, shortly before the book came out, the Guardian published an article that was ostensibly about it but which, in fact, was only about personalities (in this instance, Salman Rushdie, Ian McEwan and Julian Barnes) . . .I was rung up by the Evening Standard and Radio 4's PM programme and emailed by Newsnight—all of which wanted me to "elaborate" on what I had apparently said in the Guardian. When I pointed out that I had not said those things and that I would talk to them only if they gave me the chance to set the record straight (and not discuss personalities), they lost interest.

Ironical, because notoriety led to the publication of *Only Joking* in his adopted country (Josipovici was born in France of Russo-Italian, Romano-Levantine parentage, lived in Egypt, before finally moving to England to complete his academic education).

Josipovici objects not to one, but to all *forms* of description. Consequently, he writes dialogue. Witty, pointed, sharply drawn caricatures of characters that are sketched and lightly shaded and rarely raise an eyebrow or twitch a lip or even motion a major muscle. Talking Heads? *Only Joking.*

He is a self-confessed modernist with a mission, and that is to revive ambiguity and opacity in a text. He has acknowledged elsewhere that the point at which the writer realises her/his omnipresence and lack of authority or right to assume one forces a humility, and in this he stands shoulder-to-shoulder with Brooke-Rose and Robbe-Grillet and the pursuit of speakerless narrative sentence. The paradoxical use of present

---

* http://www.theguardian.com/books/2010/jul/28/gabriel-josipovici-dismisses-english-authors

tense (rejection of the past tense free indirect discourse mingled increasingly with an overbearing author determining the reader's interpretation of a text) with its lack of first person perspective seeks to achieve the invisibility of the author; Josipovici attains it by removing any temptation to authorial comment on the actions of the characters because a) these lack description; and b) no space exists for author intrusion when only characters speak. Or does it? Who writes? Who reads? Who speaks? *Only Joking*.

To execute his commentary, he forces his form to generate the content via the interplay of surfaces—the surface supplied by assumption, the surface reflected by familiarity, the surface depicting social nicety, and the surface concerned with personal frailty. The juxtaposition of these surfaces is what creates, ostensibly, a traditional, farcical narrative reminiscent of the films Dinner for One, Le Diner de Con, Tutto Dante, MicMacs à tire-larigo. Or Woody Allen meets John Cleese having a Roberto Benigni day. *Only Joking*.

# Steven Moore — *The Novel: An Alternative History* [2010-2013]

NATHAN GADDIS

I've been granted 500 words. Thus, a minimalist tribute from one maximalist reader to another. Steven Moore was introduced to me via his review of *Infinite Jest* which opened to me the tradition of american encyclopedic noveling. When Moore published his mammoth first volume of *The Novel: An Alternative History* I converted to Moore-ism. With the publication of his second volume, I was confirmed. Let's just think here of our Secular Scripture.

I have 500 words. Moore's *History* covers 676 novels from the Beginnings in Egypt ("The Tale of Sinuhe") to 1800 in anticipation of "a whopper about a whale"; .74 words per title. Add to this his immense reading of novels of the past 214 years and we can round up to an even 1001 novel titles included in those two volumes. Just take a gander at his various lists with emphasis on what comes forth from Rabelais' Codpiece (vI, 330f) and flows down the Shandian Stream (vII, 812ff), and the page-long catalogue of critifiction footnote (vI, 580f). Add to all of that the more than 500 words Moore writes to the effect of "were an English translation available" and "handicapped by the paucity of translations".

The thoroughness of Moore's reading has given rise to a little game : identify a novel of literary merit written before 1800 which Moore has missed. So far we've located one, *The Bohemians* by de Pelleport, fellow inmate of the Marquis de Sade. If a third volume of *The Novel* is not in the works we readers of novels have the imaginative task of continuing his history into the 19th century, through the 20th, and up to our Now. I've been adding to my version of that volume on a near daily basis.

But we can retrace Moore's steps as well, expanding on his always too narrow definition of the novel: a book-length work of fiction in prose. We want to add Herodotus, Ariosto, Burton, Gibbon, etc. And of course we can because, like Moore, our method :: "I'd rather let authors show me what a novel can be than to impose a definition on them", or, as Robert Coover has it, "a novelist *must be* nothing".

Of course for readers of innovative imaginative experimental fiction Moore's Readers' Manifesto in his introductory essay is what sells us immediately. Not that he repudiates the Hawkes enemies of fiction (plot, character, theme, &c all of which Moore includes in his analyses) but that he stresses the core of what makes fiction fiction, the "rhetorical performance", linguistic virtuosity. Perhaps we can add "passionate" to get the Barthian "passionate virtuosity". And precisely this dimension—Show me what you can do!—earns Moore a central place in Verbivoracious Press' Syllabus.

Will Self — *Walking to Hollywood* [2010]

RICHARD STRACHAN

INCHOATE COAST: IMPRESSION OF A WALK

The names of these places are a litany:
Peatdraught Bay, Battery Quarry, Inverkeithing Scrap Terminal, Bathing House Wood, Western Channel.

As a boy, the sight of machinery in water made me feel sick. The category-contrast of an oil rig spewing flame above the waves, or of a cargo ship igniting a trail of white foam in its wake, unravelled a knot in my stomach, and to look on a metal bridge across a river set a wheel of nausea spinning in my head. Iron and steel, rivets and bolts, were a kind of blasphemy to me. I couldn't find the frame of an explanation; it was just the tense confirmation of instinct. There was nothing more obscene than the idea of irrational waters breaking up against precision, the mystery of a current wending its way past the products of blueprints and machine-tools.

All this is a measure of contraction. Wrecked piers, steel hawsers, concrete blocks, bases abandoned to the underused berthings for sailboats. At each stage along the coast you can see the detritus of what used to be, where industry had grown and then dissolved. It became necessary to walk it, as if the places had no link between them until I had paced out their connections.

I was delayed by Granton Harbour, spending much of a day looking at the black water and the white sails of the boats, taking my photographs, recording digital video of wavelets lapping to the floating hawser in mid-harbour. I even found the energy for minor archival work, finding old photographs and naval records from the world wars, when the harbour had expanded to house the anti-submarine motor launches that had guarded the mouth of the Forth. HMS Claverhouse on Granton Square, formerly a hotel, was where William Golding had been trained as a newly-commissioned naval officer. I liked to think of that dark and classical mind addressing itself to shell parabolae and fuel consumption ratios. Sometimes, walking over the Road Bridge to North Queensferry, I had seen navy ships passing on the grey waves below. It was no leap to see the gunmetal hulls of war-ready craft, crews prepping the depth-charges and their 4.5 inch guns.

What began as a means to confront my nausea became something much larger than me, something I liked to think of grandiosely as a 'Project.' What I would gain when it was finished I couldn't say. Understanding, perhaps; possession, or some idea of the where the right border might lie, between the land and the sea, between sickness and health. Sometimes I worry that it has become a kind of displacement, and that what started as a way of focusing my mind away from that spiral of nausea has become a way of indulging an unhealthy need for solitude. I try to imagine someone else joining me on these long coastal walks, past all the wreckage that I only ever saw through the viewfinder. Impossible.

I raise my camera, hip-height, and think how no one puts a camera to their eye anymore. In my hands I hold the only record that it ever looked like this.

Charles Newman — In Partial Disgrace [2013]

ERIC LUNDGREN

A DEATH MASK OF CREATION

Charles Newman's final, posthumous novel, a fragment of a hugely ambitious project that consumed the last decades of his life, survives as a mosaic pieced together by his nephew Ben Ryder Howe and Jeremy Davies, his editor at Dalkey Archive and also a former student from Washington University in St. Louis, where I took one of Charlie's last classes in 2005, he a magus on his way out, myself a callow graduate student still being initiated in the first mysteries.

After putting the midwestern U.S. on the literary map as the editor of *Triquarterly* in its peak late-1960s years, he gained fame with precocious novels such as *New Axis* and *A Child's History of America*. He experienced another burst of renown in the eighties after publishing his dyspeptic essay on fiction and inflation, *The Postmodern Aura*. But Charlie had been quiet for years, and his massive project (was it a trilogy? A nine-volume spy novel?) seemed more and more unlikely to appear given the pressures of time, tobacco, and alcohol on his body. The mysterious book, supposedly involving Freud, Pavlov, and a shadow history of the 20th century, began to seem like a private myth.

In Joshua Cohen's excellent introduction to *In Partial Disgrace*, he speculates that Charlie may have in fact been a spy—how else did he manage to make several journeys to Hungary during the Cold War? But it's also easy to see how the language of spydom might have appealed to Prof. Newman, an avatar of high postmodernism occupying a 21St century English department. "To be hidden is to live well" is the motto of Cannonia's native people, the Astingi—Charlie understood as well as anyone what kind of subterfuge was required to survive, not to mention think and write, in America.

The novel, in its unfinished state, offers an oneiric pastoral to the adventurous reader. Drawn from his memories of Hungary, the beloved farm that he lost in Virginia, and his own fertile mind, the kingdom of Cannonia can also be seen as a terrestrial allegory for the imagination itself. Its serpentine, direction-changing river, the Mze, gives some idea of the wayward and elusive nature of the narrative. But *In Partial Disgrace* is also full of rich, local pleasures, set down in elegant, perfectly wrought sentences that form their own landscape.

Felix Psalmanazar, the philosophical dog trainer and country squire who stands at the heart of this book, spends his evenings at the estate of Semper Vero working on a history cum travel guide to Cannonia. His son Iulus, "Ambassador without Portfolio" and the "first great writer of the twenty-first [century]," observes him at his work:

> Nor did I know that in his hyperfastidious, shamelessly private mind, he was envisioning a nonexistent genre. For no one ever writes the book he imagines; the book becomes a death mask of creation, it has its own future and survives like a chicken dancing with its head cut off. And the spy knows this better than anyone; to write anything down is to take colossal risk. In life you can mask your actions, but once on paper, nothing can hide your mediocrity.

This book, what we have of it, is full of such poignant reminders, and is in part a meditation on its own incompleteness. But even having this partial novel feels somewhat miraculous, a deft sleight-of-hand, its creator having left us enough clues to conspire with him in his large and sustaining vision of Cannonia.

The Influences of Others

IGO WODAN

"...............*religious or morally insightful quote from an historically or culturally significant text**..............."

On the planet *Terra* in its south-eastern quadrant at the location 30°17.7756′ S 153°6.8106′ E, during the lunar cycle preceding the summer solstice of 11982 HE, a teenage boy and girl, previously students together at the local centre of academic and enterprise learning and meeting again fortuitously at a surf-and-sail festival, embarked upon a brief but doomed romance. Broken hearts and recriminations aside, the loan of the SF novel *Dune* from the one, as a substitute apology, had the most profound impact on the other.

—There's no point being a writer unless I can write like that. All that knowledge he must have acquired. That incredible assembly of ecology and economics and war and power games and politics and amazing capabilities, that mix of religion and technology, that imagination! I'll never be able to think up all those connections and plot twists and themes and different topics and make them a story. Never in a squillion light years.

—So what are you going to do?
—I dunno. Write poetry. Like Keats.
—Nobody reads poetry. Especially Keats.
—Romances then. My grandmother reads those.

***

On December 18th 1992, the beginning of an unprecedented heatwave in

---
* Which may or may not exist.

the Antipodes, the young scribbler of poetry and Barbara Cartland copycat manuscripts was given a book, *The Name of the Rose*, again by a lover of equivocal intent.

—Read this. You need some proper education. European education. Forget these silly sci-fi follies you're always touting as 'mind-blowing' and 'in depth'. This is real scholarship in fiction. Philosophy, history, symbolism, semiotics—you'll learn some Latin reading it, too—mysteries within mysteries, geography, Roman Catholic intrigues, Aristotle's lost rhetoric—

—I'm supposed to feel encouraged by this suggestion?
—You're supposed to feel loved by it.
—You're supposed to say 'I love you'!
—In this age of lost innocence, you'd laugh at me if I did.

***

Whilst playing at philosophy of science in the same year Popper and Feyerabend exited, centre stage, left . . .

" . . . no matter how many instances of white swans we may have observed, this does not justify the conclusion that *all* swans are white."

Popper

"Only when they must choose between competing theories do scientists behave like philosophers . . . scientific revolutions are inaugurated by a growing sense that an existing paradigm has ceased to function adequately in the exploration of an aspect of nature."

Kuhn

"For centuries knowledge meant proven knowledge . . . Einstein's results again turned the tables and now very few philosophers or scientists still think that scientific knowledge is, or can be, proven knowledge. But few realize that with this the whole classical structure of intellectual values falls in ruins and has to be replaced."

Lakatos

"There is no coherent *knowledge*, i.e. no uniform comprehensive account of the world and the events in it. There is no comprehensive *truth* that goes beyond an enumeration of details, but there are many *pieces of information*, obtained in different ways from different sources and collected for the benefit of the curious. The best way of presenting such knowledge is the *list*—and the oldest scientific works were indeed lists of facts, parts, coincidences, problems in several specialized domains.

Feyerabend

Thus corroborating Nietzsche: *there are no facts, only interpretation... Art is the supreme task and the truly metaphysical activity in this life.*

***

At night, by flickering candlelight, when the moths flutter towards untimely death unless the air is pregnant with the humidity of a thunderstorm, I pace the balcony recalling my friends, Justo and Jacinta, Abelho and Raimunda, and the city in which our paths crossed and our stars collided, whose unsettled history we imagined as the canvas on which we could paint our own...

Colour musings... bitumen black steaming in the aftermath of early morning rain, afternoon purplish haze of diesel motes and eucalyptus. Sea-green harbour and wind-whipped white salt spray, blotch with a red-limned sun at dusk, pavements crumbling to sepia tones... cinnamon-skinned locals strolling past dimly-lit bars in which creamy-coloured boredom smiles a fleshly invitation to pause...

I have been examining old correspondence this evening. I remember Jacinta remarking—perhaps a quote—that what gold did for Rio de Janeiro, ivory did for Maputo, and that Portugal reclaimed its colonies by exporting its financial institutions; she was rebuilding the economy with bank loans and credit cards, and I was facilitating water supplies and the removal of mines. How I loathed her for suggesting we were two sides of the same coin, exploitation, even as I loved her for awakening in me my own latent desires to abuse, to appropriate, to violate. "You are," she said, lying on her side with the rays of the the afternoon sun silhouetting her naked body, "a faux-innocent, like Durrell's Darley."

* * *

1984 is based upon the control and manipulation of productive resources (humans) through fear, although history has demonstrated that totalitarian regimes using fear reinforce their opponents—return to Nietzsche: "That which does not kill you, makes you stronger." *Brave New World* contends that productive resources are best motivated (and controlled) through pleasure—the pursuit of which trivialises or even removes the perception of inequality or imbalance. Fast-forward to 2002 and an Asian island state in which the subjugate populace is hierarchically moulded and conditioned to accept material consumption and pleasure as the status quo. Totalitarianism is dead, long live totalitarianism.

* * *

Books are no longer read, but consumed.

Books are no longer the works of artists, but the works of commodities traders.

Books are no longer devices to encourage thought, but tome-tombs of entertainment (in which to be interred while living).

Books are no longer the exploration of the uncharted territory of a writer's fecund mind, but the catalyst for the cathartic release of the reader's obstructed emotions.

Books are no longer compositions of sounds arranged in harmonious cadence, but clutches of machine-gun staccato firing monotonous blanks.

Books are no longer the mechanism by which language and communication is acquired, but the chronicles of how the globalisation of language has led to the lowest common denominator in expression (a village dialect exhibits more sophistication, even though the village inhabitants share commonality of experience and thus employ verbal abbreviations to convey meaning, than the average sentence found within the works of the money-spinner writer e.g. Rowling, Collins, Meyers, James).

* * *

"There is only one thing you write for yourself, and that is a shopping list."

Eco

* * *

The *pasticheur par excellence*: "I've always made it a point of honour never to repeat myself."

Adair

* * *

What, if at all, to distil from this brew of magi? Certainty that sufficiency of imagination as a criterion for adhering to the pursuit of the artistic vision is absent, that dictive precision or dexterity of narrative construction signifies a proficiency no more deserving of esteem than a skilled hack, that the conventional equals the mundane and abiding by its boundaries perpetuates stagnation, and that the art of *pasticheur*, while admired by some, falls short of the innovation preferred by the performer—old dancers never die, they just become choreographers.

www.ingramcontent.com/pod-product-compliance
Ingram Content Group UK Ltd.
Pitfield, Milton Keynes, MK11 3LW, UK
UKHW041302180426